ON THE DIGITAL HUMANITIES

ON THE DIGITAL HUMANITIES

HUMANITIES

ESSAYS AND PROVOCATIONS

Stephen Ramsay

University of Minnesota Press
Minneapolis
London

Portions of "The Hermeneutics of Screwing Around" were originally published as "The Hermeneutics of Screwing Around; or, What You Do with a Million Books," in *Pastplay: Teaching and Learning History with Technology,* ed. Kevin Kee, 111–20 (Ann Arbor: University of Michigan Press, 2014); reprinted with permission of the University of Michigan Press; permission conveyed through Copyright Clearance Center, Inc. Portions of "Who's In and Who's Out / On Building" were originally published as "Who's In and Who's Out" and "On Building," in *Defining Digital Humanities: A Reader,* ed. Melissa Terras, Julianne Nyhan, and Edward Vanhoutte, 239–46 (Farnham, U.K.: Ashgate, 2013).

Published by the University of Minnesota Press
111 Third Avenue South, Suite 290
Minneapolis, MN 55401–2520
http://www.upress.umn.edu

ISBN 978-1-5179-1500-1 (hc)
ISBN 978-1-5179-1501-8 (pb)

A Cataloging-in-Publication record for this book is available from the Library of Congress.

In Memoriam
Stéfan Sinclair

We want the Demon, you see, to extract from the dance of atoms only information that is genuine, like mathematical theorems, fashion magazines, blueprints, historical chronicles, or a recipe for ion crumpets, or how to clean and iron a suit of asbestos, and poetry too, and scientific advice, and almanacs, and calendars, and secret documents, and everything that ever appeared in any newspaper in the Universe, and telephone books of the future . . .

—Stanisław Lem, *The Cyberiad*

Contents

Preface and Acknowledgments

Occasionally, a student will try to take a course from me twice—Modern Drama, say, after having already taken my course on Shakespeare, or Introduction to Drama after having had me for Introduction to Literature. When calling the roll on the first day, I always say the same thing when I see a familiar name: "You must understand that most professors have only one thing to say; truly brilliant ones *might* have two. Since I am only in the first category, you should consider whether you are doomed to hear all the same observations over again: the same basic patterns of thought, the same kinds of questions, and, alas, the same jokes. You might want to reconsider." I don't recall anyone ever taking my advice. If nothing else, they know that I'm an easy A (I always have been). But I am only half joking with what I teasingly call my "repeat offenders."

This is a collection of essays written over the course of about fifteen years. They apparently pursue a variety of different topics—hermeneutics, coding, digital humanities (DH) centers, text analysis, teaching, the nature of computation, the state of the discipline—as well as offering my side in various sparring matches with other critics. But as I survey the collection, I really see only one idea—however ramified—being offered. And perhaps it is not even an idea so much as a plea: that digital humanities not forsake its connection to the humanities.

Those are fighting words, of course. And really, if one is going to have only one idea, it would be better not to yoke it to something as inchoate and resistant to firm definition as "the humanities." For if anything distinguishes the contemporary humanities disciplines, it is a desire to be confused with some other kind of discipline. Thus the analytical philosopher confesses to being secretly a mathematician; the "place-based" literary critic advocates for what most still call geography; what the literary critic calls "theory," most call "philosophy";

any number of humanistic subspecialties concerned with matters of race and gender start to look like any number of social science disciplines. Is it any wonder that so many humanities disciplines would, as the end of the millennium approached, decide to become a form of computer science?

I have never really disagreed with those who think this is going a bit too far. Some disciplines add the prefix *critical* when they want to distinguish themselves from more empirical forms of social study (critical geography, critical race theory); others add the suffix *science* when they want to go the other way (political science, data science). But no serious computer scientist, whatever the names and appearances, thinks the discipline is an empirical science on analogy with physics or chemistry. Computer science is the study of a certain kind of mathematical formalism ("computation," broadly) with consequences enormous enough to warrant a separate floor. All the first "computer scientists" were mathematicians, and many remain essentially so. The humanities and social sciences have always been fellow travelers; alliances and interdisciplines were and are inevitable. But what is Hecuba to Huffman coding? Barely anything at all. At the root of subjects like compiler theory, machine learning, concurrency, and programming language research are questions and concerns that do not resemble those of humanistic inquiry in any way, and it is rare for a digital humanist to engage with these matters in any but the most applied and instrumental manner. No wonder so many regard the entire enterprise as fundamentally wrongheaded.

I have maintained a constant fascination with these more rarefied aspects of computation throughout my career, and I offer only the most halfhearted apologies for the naive enthusiasms that have sometimes arisen from this preoccupation. I might be too fearful of ridicule to say out loud (as Steve Jobs did throughout his career) that a computer is a "bicycle for the mind," but I think I have always secretly believed that it is "the most remarkable tool we've ever come up with."[1] I routinely describe it to my undergraduate programming students as "the greatest of all machines—a machine for making machines." The raw theoretical matter of computation has always seemed to me a kind of miracle, and even seeing that miracle darkened and despoiled by the forces of late capitalism hasn't entirely diminished my faith. But at no point have I ever imagined that there is any kind of natural connection between humanistic inquiry and computation. In fact, early on, I came to believe that whatever utility computers might have for humanists arises precisely from the unnatural character of the relationship. As these pages will make plain, I've been at war with those who say otherwise—anyone who would like to say that computers bring "objectivity" or "rigor" to the humanities—for a long time. And while some would say that such people make for easy targets, I have found the positive formulations much more elusive.

Most of the essays in this volume began as talks and are here rerendered and expanded (often quite heavily) for on-the-page consumption. Every one of them, it seems to me, circles around this "one thing" to various degrees. Some belong so much to their historical moment that I briefly considered creating a section called "Period Pieces." I decided against that not because I regard anything here as timeless (I doubt that such a thing exists) but because I think what Matthew K. Gold once called "the Digital Humanities moment" is nearly always either an observation about the past or a hope for the future.[2]

When I started in the field, there seemed to me a marked division between those who regarded digital humanities (or "humanities computing," as it was then called) as a twenty-five-year project. The old "analog" humanities needed an upgrade, and digital humanities was precisely the strategic plan for making that happen (when it finally did, there would be no need for the term, since *humanities* and *digital humanities* would be synonyms). Others thought that a digital humanist was a subspecialist—like a medievalist or a paleographer—and that it only remained for digital humanities to reach sufficient disciplinary definition (along with funding, centers, departments, professorships, conferences, journals, and all the rest) to take its rightful place in the academy. The one thought constantly of what would come after DH; the other was always chasing after DH.

The matter is discussed in far less Manichaean terms today, but the essential tension remains. I don't know that there is any field as anxious about where it has been and as concerned about what it will be tomorrow as DH. The volume in which Gold first spoke of "the Digital Humanities moment" (*Debates in the Digital Humanities*), after all, went on to be a series—an almost annual metadiscussion of hopes, fears, criticisms, anxieties, gatekeeping, and tent-expansion projects. Were digital humanities not so eager to know itself, I doubt that I would have been invited to speak so often and at such length on questions of disciplinary definition. It occurred to me a while ago that I could fill a book with the fruits of such generous invitations, and here I have done so.

But not by myself, of course. Each one of these essays is associated in my mind with dozens of people. Very often I was being welcomed by hosts I had never met but who went on to become cherished friends and colleagues. It is very hard to imagine having written this book without the generous feedback offered over the course of so many years by my hosts. And so it is with pleasure that I recall the thanks I owe to Craig Bellamy, Elisa Beshero-Bondar, Jamie "Skye" Bianco, David Birnbaum, Jeremy Boggs, Ryan Cordell, Andreas Fickers, Julia Flanders, Steven E. Jones, Alison Langmead, Andrew Mactavish, Willard McCarty, Jerome McGann, Martin Mueller, Elli Mylonas, Brad Pasanek, Geoffrey Rockwell, Brian Rosenblum, John Unsworth, and Annette Vee. Certainly, the book would have been impossible without the support, encouragement, and sage advice of some very dear friends: Matt Cohen, Brian Croxall, Amanda French, Mike Furlough, Matt Gold, Shana Kimball, Matt Kirschenbaum, Kari Kraus, Beth Nowviskie, Jason Rhody, Lisa Rhody, Mark Sample, Erin Templeton, Ethan Watrall, and Sarah Werner. The reader has been spared a great many bad ideas, rhetorical dead ends, and other infelicities by the candid advice of Kathleen Fitzpatrick, Tom Scheinfeldt, and Brian Pytlik-Zillig; the eagle-eyed copyediting skills of Ziggy Snow; the lovely text composition of Wendy Holdman; the thorough indexing of Denise Carlson; and the prudence and good sense of my editors at the University of Minnesota Press, Doug Armato and Zenyse Miller. As always, I have June Griffin to thank for most things.

It is bittersweet to dedicate this volume to the memory of one of my oldest friends in the field: Stéfan Sinclair, whose untimely death in 2020 made an already difficult year seem far worse. It lessens my grief a bit, though, to know that since he would never have grown weary of poking fun at me for such a gesture, it does allow me one last joyful laugh with him.

Textual Behavior in the Human Male

My title, of course, refers to the infamous Kinsey report *Sexual Behavior in the Human Male,* first published in 1948.

The Kinsey report is, like *Harry Potter, The Omnivore's Dilemma,* and the book of Job, one of those books you feel you've read even if you haven't actually read it. Its general outlines and conclusions, and the national sense of scandal that ensued, are well known even after seventy years. When you do sit down to read it, though, the most shocking thing isn't its prurience or its candor but its easy, approachable tone. It sounds like this:

> The English people are more or less justly reputed to be the most completely clothed people in the world, and Americans have been slow in breaking with English tradition. The American visitor to foreign lands is often amazed at the exposure which is allowed in some other cultures, and he criticizes it on moral grounds. The nudity of the French burlesque is ascribed to the "low morality" of the Frenchmen as a group; and although an approach is made to the same sort of display in American burlesque, the institution here does not achieve the same free acceptance of complete nudity which the original French has.[1]

On kissing:

> The lower level male [Kinsey is speaking here of lower socio economic class] considers [deep kissing] to be dirty, filthy, and a source of disease, although he may drink from a common cup which hangs on the water pail, and he may utilize common utensils in eating and drinking. Obviously, the arguments, at both levels,

have nothing to do with the real issues. They are rationalizations of mores which place taboos upon mouth contacts for reasons which only the student of custom can explain.[2]

This tone—learned, somewhat detached, but entirely approachable and plainspoken—is something like the tone assumed by the generation that produced Max Weber, Vannevar Bush, Claude Leví-Strauss, Émile Durkheim, Walter Ong, Clifford Geertz, and even, in his less strident moments, Marshall McLuhan. No self-respecting sociologist would write like this today.

Yet all of this almost-belletristic prose is accompanied by hundreds of earnest-looking graphs and tables that mark it, unmistakably, as of a piece with modern science. You have to wade through a full 150 pages of detailed methodological discussion to get to the good parts, and even when you get there, the text wavers back and forth between cold data and hot description. One minute, he sounds like Lewis Mumford; the next minute, he sounds like (or, rather, looks like) a man delivering a report on the hydrology of the American Midwest. But make no mistake, Kinsey seems to say, all of this is science. And that means something very particular. Here's Kinsey again, in the introduction to the work:

> The present study . . . represents an attempt to accumulate an objectively determined body of fact about sex which strictly avoids social or moral interpretations of the fact. Each person who reads this report will want to make interpretations in accordance with his understanding of moral values and social significances; but that is not part of the scientific method and, indeed, scientists have no special capabilities for making such evaluations. . . . This is first of all a report on what people do, which raises no question of what they should do, or what kinds of people do it. It is the story of the sexual behavior of the human male, as we find him.[3]

The extraordinary naivete of this paragraph is entirely patent to any humanist. The human male "as we find him"? Each person "will want to make interpretations"? It is scarcely necessary to rehearse the problems with such notions, and for the record, absolutely no one bought it. In fact, the Kinsey report bears the Library of Congress subject heading "United States—Moral Conditions."

But Kinsey's insistence that this is "just the facts" is not simply a moment of wishful thinking—a dodge intended to tamp down the raging criticisms that he knew would come, and which did come from all quarters. It belongs, rather, to a moment in history that starts around the turn of the century, continues until just after the Second World War, and arguably occurs in more sublimated forms up until the present day. What Kinsey is struggling with is the scientization of the humanities.

Sex and the erotic were, after all, for most of the history of the West, *our* department—which is to say, the province of art and of humanistic inquiry. Freud barely even attempts to scientize his subject matter. A great number of Freud's basic ideas form the ground truths of modern psychology, but his hermeneutical framework lives on mainly in English departments. Vladimir Nabokov's legendary quip—"Let the credulous and the vulgar continue to believe that all mental woes can be cured by a daily application of old Greek myths to their private parts"—is not far off the mark, inasmuch as Freud's basic method is fully embedded in the traditions of literary criticism.[4] The same might be said of Marx, whose most scientific influence is probably Lucretius.

But Kinsey appears at a time when nearly all the subjects of humanistic concern are being reexamined as questions susceptible to scientific methodology. What is the meaning of work? What is the imagination? How do I live a good and fruitful life? What is love? Ian F. McNeely and Lisa Wolverton, in their book *Reinventing Knowledge,* locate the rise of the social sciences in the twentieth century precisely in the attempt to explore such questions using scientific methods:

The ability of modern science to manipulate and master nature, to command public esteem, and to change public behavior arose from the synergy of a craft workshop fused with a disciplinary seminar. . . . Social scientists rose to influence by applying laboratory techniques to places where people now learned, worked, and lived. Disciplines such as economics, sociology, and anthropology were already developing around traditional philological methods. Writers like Adam Smith, Max Weber, and Émile Durkheim provided a body of canonical texts for endless analysis, and written sources like government statistics and travel reports gave their acolytes the means to produce new scholarship. . . . Social scientists

became intelligence testers, efficiency experts, scientific philan-
thropists, and much else besides. Humanists transformed into scientists, they took their white-coated counterparts as a model. They
measured and quantified; they indoctrinated cadres of experts in
experimental methods; and they crossed into the public domain
bearing "objective," impartial findings meant to effect widespread
social change.[5]

The catalog of results, even in the less obviously appalling instances—
Hitler was exceedingly fond of such methods—is the sort of thing that
makes humanists cringe.

Standardized testing began with these early forays into scientized
humanism, with the result that "every human being, whatever his or
her particular constellation of intellectual faults and fortes, carries a
two- or three-digit 'intelligence quotient' (IQ), largely invariant over
a lifetime, that denotes his or her inherent mental capacity."[6] Students of Taylorism, armed with stopwatch, clipboard, and camera,
attempted to break every factory worker's movements into their con-
stituent parts in search of efficiency. Statistics became the principal
tool wielded by large philanthropic institutions, so that attempts to
cool race relations and eradicate poverty could be based not on traditional dialectical methods and religious philosophies but on cold,
hard facts. The Kinsey report itself was funded mainly with Rockefel-
ler money.

We cringe not because we dispute the facts that more modern instantiations of these methods provide but because we are suspicious
of the ability of facts to translate into answers to questions that have
persisted—literally for centuries—within the humanistic disciplines.
The integrity of Kinsey's work as science was sharply criticized almost
immediately. Yet in the end, Kinsey's conclusions still stand. Many
more people masturbate than say they do; the range of sexual experience differs according to both race and class; *homosexual* and *hetero-
sexual* (terms that Kinsey studiously avoided as ontic descriptors)
merely mark the poles of a broad spectrum of sexual behaviors and
feelings experienced by most humans over the course of their lives.
These were, in Kinsey's estimation, the facts of the case. If he cannot
hold himself to dispassionate dilation of those facts, it is not because
such a project is impossible but rather because there was no available discourse for relating scientific facts to humanistic conclusions.

The ancient pornographer knew precisely "what he actually does." But what does it mean?

There are several varieties of digital humanities that offend no one. The student of human culture can hardly object to the work of those who have labored tirelessly, these last few decades, to bring the written artifacts of human experience online. The study of digital culture itself—media studies and its various offshoots—is likewise so consistent with the ordinary hermeneutical methods of the humanities as to be barely noticeable as a "new thing." Even those suspicious of work in educational technology will concede the general utility of such research; the fact that most course management systems are terrible is not usually taken to mean that the entire project of bringing technology to bear on teaching should be roundly condemned.

What strikes fear in our hearts are those who greet with great enthusiasm the possibility of using computers in order to engage in the quantitative analysis of cultural artifacts. People, to put it plainly, like me. My own career development as a digital humanist is very much like what McNeely and Wolverton describe. Like the early social scientists, I was trained entirely in the art of the seminar and in the deployment of theoretical frameworks, which, though touted as new, were methodologically descended from dialectical and philological traditions that began during the rise of the modern university in nineteenth-century France and Germany. Becoming a digital humanist meant—and still means—learning to operate within a laboratory environment. A digital center today is, in fact, very much like a chemistry or biology lab. Knowledge is conveyed not primarily through free-flowing, seminar-style discussion but through collective and collaborative mastery of complicated equipment and difficult methodologies. "Thing knowledge" is essential.

We encounter, too, some of the objections that were leveled at nineteenth-century science, which (we should recall) had great difficulty inserting itself into the university. In telling the story of modern science, we are apt to focus on resistance to the work of scientists like Darwin, whose conclusions (much like Kinsey's) challenged numerous assumptions that had been in place for centuries. But the more immediate problem for the likes of Pasteur or Lavoisier is that their work looked for all the world like plumbing. Laboratories, for most of the nineteenth century, were housed in people's homes and relied heavily on developing the skills necessary for fabricating and manipulating equipment for the purpose of making accurate measurements—something that had always been a nonacademic craft skill. From the standpoint of the faculty at Paris, nothing could be more base. Even the words Lavoisier used to describe his work—"carbonate," "nitrate," "sulfate"—seemed barbaric to the French intelligentsia and presumably rolled off their tongues much as the jargon of computation does today for many members of the humanities faculty.[7]

And what is it, precisely, that we digital humanists are fabricating? Susan Hockey, one of the pioneers of digital humanities in its modern form, offers a definition of our principal toolset that is as uncontroversial as it is dispiriting:

> Computers can assist with the study of literature in a variety of ways, some more successful than others. . . . Computer-based tools are especially good for comparative work, and here some simple statistical tools can help to reinforce the interpretation of the material. These studies are particularly suitable for testing hypotheses or for verifying intuition. They can provide concrete evidence to support or refute hypotheses or interpretations which have in the past been based on human reading and the somewhat serendipitous noting of interesting features.[8]

The echoes of Kinsey should be obvious: the text as we find it—an objectively determined body of fact about text that strictly avoids social or moral interpretations of the text. Each person who reads our work will want to make interpretations in accordance with their understanding of moral values and social significances; but that is not part of the digital humanities and, indeed, digital humanists have no special capabilities for making such evaluations.

The genealogy I have been tracing suggests a clear teleology for digital humanities. Digital humanities, which, in its data-centric forms, is composed of a set of practices that centers on tool building and instrumental methods of analysis, represents yet another attempt to scientize the humanities. It will struggle mightily to insert itself fully into the academy, but once it does, it will make a clean break with its more purely contemplative past. The social sciences are not "the sciences"; *digital* humanities will not be the humanities. A few years ago, I was at a conference on data mining in the humanities. During one of the breaks, a quite prominent historian—well known for his use of quantitative methods—leaned over to me and said, "I used to be a historian. Now I'm a social scientist."

The question I'd like to propose is simply this: How do we prevent this from happening?

Some, it should be said, would very much like this to happen and see digital humanities as the way forward. Jonathan Gottschall, in a 2008 editorial in the *Boston Globe,* describes the field of literary studies as "moribund, aimless, and increasingly irrelevant to the concerns not only of the 'outside world,' but also to the world inside the ivory tower." The solution is one that even C. P. Snow would have found provocative:

> I think there is a clear solution to this problem. Literary studies should become more like the sciences. Literature professors should apply science's research methods, its theories, its statistical tools, and its insistence on hypothesis and proof. Instead of philosophical despair about the possibility of knowledge, they should embrace science's spirit of intellectual optimism. If they do, literary studies can be transformed into a discipline in which real understanding of literature and the human experience builds up along with all of the words.
>
> This proposal may distress many of my colleagues, who may worry that adopting scientific methods would reduce literary study to a branch of the sciences. But if we are wise, we can admit that the sciences are doing many things better than we are, and gain from studying their successes, without abandoning the things that make literature special.[9]

I, for one, react to this idea with horror. I'll take philosophical despair any day of the week.

Let me say that I am precisely the sort of person who should be clamoring for this mystical singularity in which the humanities sloughs off its ancient proclivity for free-flowing discussion of questions without answers and embraces the optimistic joy of scientific positivism. I have spent my whole career as an English professor studying computers. I consider myself entirely fluent in at least a dozen programming languages; I have learned the arcana of statistical mathematics; I can hold my own in a conversation with any computer scientist; and I spend most of my days either building tools or teaching unsuspecting English and history majors how to do the same (sometimes in the Department of Computer Science). What's more, my methods are more or less exactly like those of Gottschall, whose work is fascinating and focuses mainly on computational analysis of text. I am an enthusiastic and active member of the revolution.

But my own sense of what makes the humanities "special" is its alternative ways of knowing and talking. I have nothing but the highest respect for scientific ways of knowing and talking, social or otherwise. But a world in which the mysteries of the human condition are unfolded without the methodologies of the humanities seems to me a poorer world. So when I say, "How do we prevent this from happening?" I really mean, "How do we move forward with the wondrous tools and methods of digital technology while still remaining faithful to ourselves?"

Because the tools are, indeed, wondrous.

Here's a list of English novels created by David Hoover, a professor of English at NYU, a longtime member of the digital humanities community, a brilliant text analysis scholar, and someone with whom I disagree on a quite regular basis:

William Faulkner, *Light in August*
Henry James, *The Ambassadors*
Bram Stoker, *Dracula*
D. H. Lawrence, *Sons and Lovers*
Oscar Wilde, *The Picture of Dorian Gray*
Virginia Woolf, *To the Lighthouse*
Willa Cather, *My Ántonia*
H. G. Wells, *The War of the Worlds*
Jack London, *The Sea Wolf*
Mark Twain, *Pudd'nhead Wilson*
Rudyard Kipling, *Kim*
Sinclair Lewis, *Main Street*[10]

The list was produced by writing some code that orders texts in terms of "vocabulary richness," which Hoover defines, for the purposes of this experiment, as the number of different words per fifty-thousand-word block. That is to say, it organizes novels in terms of how "wide" or how varied the vocabulary is in a particular author.

I've shown this list to lots of people over the years, including quite a few professors who are familiar with every novel on the list. Most have an easy time placing either Henry James or William Faulkner at the top of this list, perhaps alongside either Mark Twain or Oscar Wilde. *Kim* and *The Sea Wolf*, both books that are frequently offered to young adult readers, presumably belong somewhere near the bottom. Perhaps you are thinking of this slightly differently, with well-conceived—if only briefly considered—arguments for where the books belong on the spectrum of vocabulary richness.

But the truth is that no one I've ever showed it to—including the English professors—has gotten it remotely correct. This list, you see, is in *ascending* order of vocabulary richness: Faulkner and James at the bottom in terms of rich vocabulary, Kipling and Lewis at the top.

And then it starts. The first objection is to the notion of "richness," which, you'll recall, is clearly stipulated when the problem is presented. Most will complain that "richness" has nothing at all to do with the number of different words, though when I ask what "richness" is, it's as if I asked them about something entirely ineffable. Others react by quickly explaining to me why these results are clearly correct, despite having just given me the wrong answer. Such explanations can be quite elaborate, very well thought out, and entirely enlightening, but they're delivered in a tone that says, "Yes, yes, of course. I knew that." Other text analysis practitioners will immediately begin talking about sample size, tokenization, and other technical aspects of the methodology (as if to say, "I would have known that, if you had conducted the experiment properly!").

The disposition of the researcher is instructive as well. Hoover, who created the list, is solidly of the positivist party. In an article entitled "The End of the Irrelevant Text: Electronic Texts, Linguistics, and Literary Theory," he writes:

Much high theory is deeply influenced by ideas about the instability of the sign and the tendency of texts to disintegrate under critical pressure, ideas most closely associated with the late Jacques Derrida. Jerome McGann, for example, champions the game-like, "fundamentally subjective character of . . . criticism" and asks "What if the question isn't 'how could he [the critic] take himself or his ideas seriously' but 'why should he take himself or his ideas seriously'?" Stanley Fish emphasizes the reader's role, attacking the idea that texts have meaning at all—arguing that the only links that exist between the text and its interpretation are those that are "fashioned in response to the demands of the reading experience." Critical approaches like these and a more general distrust of the sign/signified link within literary theory helped to produce a climate inhospitable to text-analysis and stylistics.[11]

Hoover's project, briefly, is to destroy this arrant nonsense with the power of technology. You thought you knew what was going on? Well, you don't. I will admit to a certain guilty pleasure in showing people this list; it is a bit of a gotcha, after all. I usually don't mention my own reaction when the experiment was conducted on me: astonishment, followed by the irresistible urge to go try it on someone else.

But it's the contours of the resulting conversation, and our sense of what it is we're doing with this kind of work, that fascinates me—in particular, the ways in which reactions to Hoover's list closely resemble reactions to the Kinsey report. We want to talk about methodology, or we want to talk about how we knew it all along. We want to stand back and present results as "the facts," or we want to critique the notion of fact itself. We become, in other words, something like humanists transformed into scientists, taking our white-coated counterparts as a model. What is missing from such conversations, it seems to me, is actual humanistic discussion.

Let's begin by admitting that Hoover's list is probably correct as an experimental observation. It might be flawed in dozens of ways, but I suspect it isn't, and no matter how many experiments we conduct, we're eventually going to have to accept or reject conclusions that are, like both scientific and humanistic conclusions, largely the result of inductive reasoning. Let us also admit that these results surprise us; it's just not the way we think of these books. Then, instead of trying to explain it all away as knowledge that is somehow already fully tractable within our current paradigms, let us ask, "What on earth does this mean?"

It might suggest peculiar mappings between the way books are un-

derstood in general as cultural objects and how that comes to influence the way they are experienced by individual readers. It might lead
us toward a deeper understanding of reading itself and of "richness"
as something that is experienced conceptually but then thought to
inhere in textuality in some more literal manner. It raises any number
of questions about the evolution of English style, which is only dimly
understood even by experienced linguists. Most importantly, it suggests study of our own discursive practices—not only interrogation of
our critical paradigms but further awareness of the way we conduct
discussion within those paradigms.

Over the years, my work has become a quest for meaningful astonishment, and I had a particularly stirring moment several years ago
while working on Virginia Woolf's 1931 novel *The Waves*.

> [*The Waves*] consists of a series of monologues that trace the lives
> of six friends from early childhood to old age, each monologue
> (beginning always with "Susan said" or "Bernard said") telling
> the characters' stories at seven distinct stages of their lives. Yet
> "story" is far too strong a word for their ruminations. The char-
> acters recount only a few of the sorts of events one would expect
> to see forming the basis of plot in a conventional narrative. They
> speak about different things and have different perspectives on
> the world, but they all speak in roughly the same manner, and do
> so from childhood to adulthood—employing, as one critic puts
> it, "the same kind of sentence rhythms and similar kinds of image
> patterns" throughout. Some critics have suggested that there are
> differences that lie along the axis of gender or along a rift separat-
> ing the more social characters from the more solitary ones, but in
> the end, one has the sense of an overall unity running against the
> perspectival conceit that frames the narrative.[12]

This is precisely the sort of problem that attracts text analysis practitioners. So a graduate student of mine (Sara Steger, now at the University of Georgia) and I began running classification and clustering
algorithms on Woolf's text, precisely to see if there were similitudes
that are hard to arrive at using, to borrow Hockey's phrase, "ordinary
reading." The work was going well, mostly because we spent most of
our time trying to understand what it was we were looking at. On a

lark, we decided to pose a simple question: What are the words that the women in the novel use but which none of the men use? Here's what we found:

shoes	antlers	cotton	stockings
lambert	bowl	diamonds	wash
million	breath	rushes	
pirouetting	coarse	soften	

We then did the same for the men:

boys	included	board	course
possible	ourselves	novel	torture
ends	alas	reason	forgotten
church	inflict	brake	crucifix
sentences	poetry	observe	troubling
everybody	approach	respect	friend
Larpent	irrelevant	burnt	distinctions
tortures	power	oppose	use
feeling	background	telephone	God
office	knew	central	distracted
united	arms	pointing	waste
felt	baker	waistcoat	king
rhythm	language	certainly	doctor
weep	destiny	beak	watched
heights	banks	chose	notice
wheel	Latin	sheer	ease
able	letters	chaos	willows
however	became	cinders	ordinary
banker	meeting	story	edges
accepted	lord	difficult	works
hundred	block	clamour	
Brisbane	neat	suffering	
act	poet	endure	

Did you just gasp? So did we. Some critics find this list terribly upsetting—convinced that I've done something wrong. Others feel absolutely confirmed by it (the sexism of the Western canon, pace Gottschall, writ large). But if you're anything like the many scholars

I've shown this to over the years, your immediate reaction is to re-solve either disposition with further experimentation. Perhaps the women are more isolated? Or their vocabulary is more rich (how do we do that richness thing again)? Most of the questions that abound begin with, "Have you tried . . . ?" Have you tried it with other novels, other time periods, other character breakdowns, by author gender, by genre, or with Jane Austen? If you're thinking this way, perhaps you've caught the digital humanities bug. It is my pleasure to wel-come you. But I must ask: What is it that we are trying to know? Are we trying to find an *answer*? And if so, what is the question? Do we imagine that such further experiments would resolve long-standing questions about gender and language? Do we really want those ques-tions resolved?

That last question may seem slightly perverse, but I believe that, in the end, what is most distinct about humanistic inquiry is its re-sistance toward final answers. It is the goal of the seminar to answer questions, but mostly by proposing them more fruitfully. The humani-ties wants for itself a world that is more complex than we thought—a sense of the human experience as deeper and more surprising. We are in search of a conversation, really, and the things that have always sustained that conversation are the artifacts of the human experience (especially, though not exclusively, written artifacts).

In 2015, the Text Creation Partnership released into the public do-main nearly every title from the first two centuries of English print culture. The Perseus Digital Library right now contains nearly the entire extant corpus of ancient Greek. The digital Library of Latin Texts contains nearly every important work written in Latin between 240 BCE and the Second Vatican Council. In 2019, Google Books announced that it has scanned over forty million books in over four hundred languages.[13] I could go on. These resources are so new that nearly every question we ask of them is one that has never been asked before—largely because without digital tractability, our only real op-tion was to read them all (an impossible task, by any measure).

It is customary to say that such wonders will transform the humani-ties, but that is not at all clear to me. The technical requirements for the study of large-scale corpora are often quite significant (though I should mention that my students are writing programs like Hoover's and mine within a few weeks). But that is not even the limiting factor. The limiting factor, it seems to me, is how (and, perhaps, whether) we decide to remain humanists in the face of such abundance. We can do what we've always done; we're interested in talking about books, and now we will read them online. The other option, though, seems to me the more exciting one: learning to read anew using the tools of the new technology. At least some of us need to become programmers, tool builders, data scientists. But many more of us need to decide to invite the new texts that result from these activities—frequency lists, visualizations, n-grams, maps, data mining results, and much more—into our ongoing conversation.

That might mean, ironically, learning to write like Kinsey—oscillating back and forth between essay and data, belle lettres and *numerique*—without the pretense of scientific positivism. Perhaps then we can create works that attempt to accumulate a subjective body of rumination about text that strictly embraces social or moral interpretations of the text. Each person who reads such a report will want to make interpretations in accordance with his or her understanding. That is part of the humanistic method, and indeed, humanists have unique capabilities in making such evaluations.

Data and Interpretation

The word *data* feels right when we're describing lists of things: numbers, words, frequencies, properties. It feels wrong to speak of, say, *The Pickwick Papers* as a "dataset," unless we convert it from its present formation into a list of numbers, words, frequencies, or properties. We do not consider these new formations to be *The Pickwick Papers,* and yet as we transform the data further, into visualizations and explanations, we stop speaking about data, per se, and begin to speak of "what the data show" or "what the data mean," as if to say that the data can be made to show or mean as stories (like the story with which we began) show things and mean things. While we might continue to use the word *data* while showing and meaning, the word itself remains a placeholder for when there's much more to say, something essential that needs to be supplied, a point yet to be made. There might be much more we want to say about the thing we do refer to, absent any further transformation, as *"The Pickwick Papers,"* but we don't regard Dickens's novel—or any novel, really—as an object that cannot stand without further narrative.

Further narrative is possible, of course. Literary criticism is precisely this further narrative, and often it is presented as the illumination of something otherwise hard to discern, and not in plain sight for all to see. But we think of data as something that requires such interventions. Without supplementary narrative (one might argue) data really doesn't "mean" anything—or worse, can mean anything at all. Data might even be regarded as a bit dangerous, and for either reason.

There is a website called FOUND Magazine that is not usually thought of as a data aggregation site but which seems to me to fit the definition perfectly.[1] Essentially, it is a site devoted to found objects from the daily lives of anonymous individuals: love letters, birthday cards, kids' homework assignments, ticket stubs, poetry on napkins, doodles. Typically, such items are picked up off the ground, scanned, and submitted to the site. In other words, not just love letters, birth-day cards, and poems, but love letters in which the lovers are entirely unknown, birthday cards entirely cut off from the lives of the people celebrating, poetry that is not merely anonymous but presumably lost and perhaps abandoned. All can be found on FOUND. But the great glorious treasure of FOUND, in my opinion, is its lists (see Figures 1–3).

Surely, this is data. And yet these lists so instantly become narrative that it's hard to say—maybe impossible to say—precisely when it stops being the former and becomes the latter. An entire world of associations is evoked by these spare lists. And what's more, it is pre-

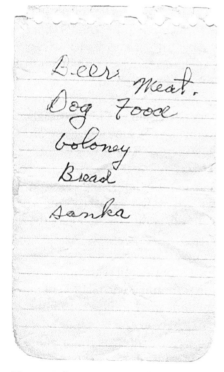

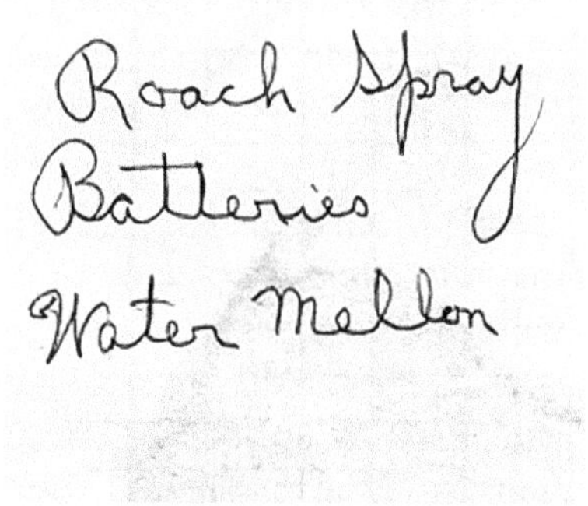

Figure 2. An anonymous shopping list. Image from FOUND, foundmagazine.com.

Figure 1. An anonymous shopping list. Image from FOUND, foundmagazine.com.

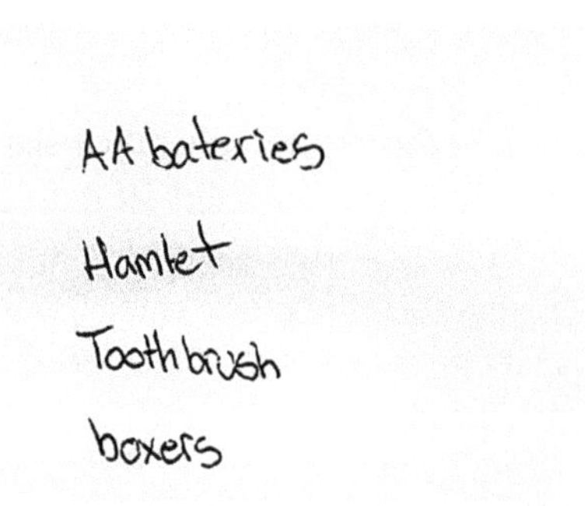

Figure 3. A list of essential items? Image from FOUND, foundmagazine.com.

cisely the spareness of the lists—the complete absence of context—
that gives rise to the narrative. Do we not know exactly the sort of
person who buys "beer, meat, dog food, baloney, bread, Sanka"?
Well, not really. If pressed, we might say "not at all." But who can help
imagining this person anyway? "Damn it, there's roaches everywhere.
Or at least, I think there are. The flashlight's dead. Watermelon . . ."
Or maybe it's not quite that well formed in our minds, and it's just
the juxtaposition of two eminently practical things with something
that is joyous and associated with summer that makes it funny and
somehow poignant.

Another appears to be a receipt from the Toronto Public Library
(see Figure 4). Again, how hard it is to avoid "drawing conclusions"
from the "data." And consider how the world that is suggested would
expand or contract if we added or removed titles. Men, women,
and . . . what? Figure 5 is perhaps a New Year's resolution. But then, it
could have been a list—"draw, paint, DVD, book, studio"—in which
case the exuberant micronarrative might be regarded as an interpretation of the data.

```
            Eatonville
        08 SEP 2007 04:39pm
        Toronto Public Library

The unexpected legacy of divorce :
39014030177683        Due: 29 SEP 2007 *

The dangerous book for boys /
37131075317370        Due: 29 SEP 2007 *

Second chances : men, women, and
37131043262880        Due: 29 SEP 2007 *

Surviving schizophrenia : a manual
37131058423187        Due: 29 SEP 2007 *

Music theory for dummies /
37131070447321        Due: 29 SEP 2007 *
Items in group: 2


   Sept. 8th - International Literacy Day
        Share the gift of literacy
     Volunteer and make a difference
```

Figure 4. A receipt from the Toronto Public Library. Image from FOUND, foundmagazine.com.

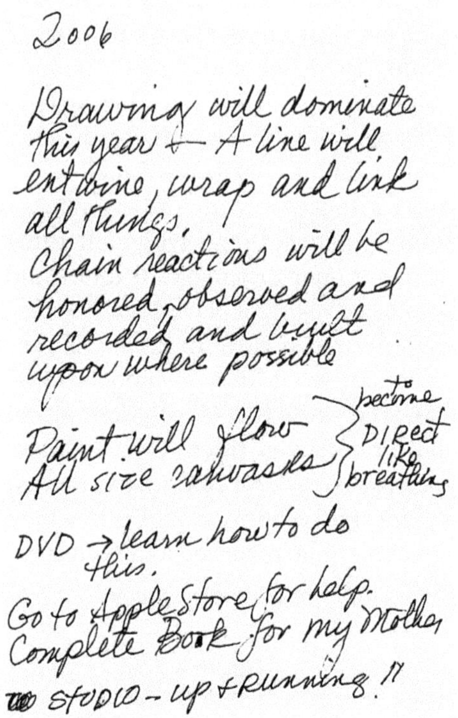

2006

Drawing will dominate
this year — A line will
entwine, wrap and link
all things.
Chain reactions will be
honored, observed and
recorded and built
upon where possible

Paint will flow } become
All size canvasses } Direct
} like breathing

DVD → learn how to do
this.
Go to Apple Store for help.
Complete Book for my Mother
to STUDIO – up & running!!

Figure 5. A note to self? Image from FOUND, foundmagazine.com.

I don't know if anyone has ever noticed one of their lost items on FOUND and written in to provide an explanation. I suppose the "beer, meat, dog food" person could end all speculation by stepping forward and telling us what the data mean. But that does not mean that the data are meaningless without that (presumably) authoritative viewpoint. If anything, the data are *more* meaningful without it.

But this is nothing, really. As humans, we possess the remarkable ability to gather the available sensory data and see things that (the expert interpreters will tell us) aren't there: an image of the Virgin Mary on a slice of toast or a face on the surface of Mars. The phenomenon is sometimes referred to as *pareidolia*. The more general term, which is not restricted to sounds and images, is *apophenia*. Both are neologisms referring to the same phenomenon—the tendency to discern meaning and connection among unrelated or even random data—and both terms were coined to describe the early stages of mental illness.[2]

Unfortunately, one of the few verifiable distinctions between the apparently natural tendency to detect patterns and the onset of psychosis is whether others see what you see. You may well agree that that cloud looks like a rabbit but be unable to see (as in the famous case of the mathematician John Nash) that people are trying to communicate with you through the colors of men's neckties.[3] And there is a lot of space between. The gambler convinced that there is pattern and order to the numbers on lottery tickets may be deluded, but not necessarily in the clinical sense. And in all cases, this propensity for pattern and order appears to be an essential cognitive ability. That we are able to see familiar faces in a crowd (rightly or wrongly) undoubtedly served an important survival function in the evolution of humans. After all, if you hear a rustle in the grass and think it might be the sound of a tiger, that might save your life. We have even taught computers to do it. When facial recognition software mistakenly interprets the front of a car as a face, we call it a bug. But if that's what it is, it is clearly also a "bug" in the human mind.

The trouble, of course, is that all of this shows up not merely in clouds and lottery numbers but in literary criticism. *Dracula* is a book about a violent, Eastern European aristocrat who comes back from the dead during the British fin de siècle and proceeds to run around England sucking the blood of Victorian virgins. Literary critics, predictably, detect a metaphor here—one that undoubtedly involves Freud and/or Marx and that variously attributes this narrative to any number of unconscious fears among late-century Britons. Repressed motives aside, Bram Stoker himself appears to have been trying to write a scary story in the typical (and popular) Gothic mold.

So what's going on here? Apophenia? Well, no. *Dracula* is hardly random data. Yet our students might quietly murmur that we're "reading too much into it" when we suggest that the novel might be a response to the New Woman, a book rife with fears of racial mixing and gender fluidity, or an effluvium of repressed homosexuality (to mention only a few of the more influential readings of the novel). But what, in the case of data, is this "it" into which we're reading too much? The novel—or rather, its "after-narrative," its explanatory formation—is possibly more interesting without Stoker. Then again, Mars is surely more interesting with a face on it. What does it mean to say that *Dracula* is not *really* about sublimated fear of a dying aristocracy coming back to life? What does it mean to say that there isn't *really* a face on Mars?

Claiming some kind of epistemological affinity between New Historicism and the discernment of sacred images on toast might suggest a freewheeling approach to data—fine enough for anonymous shopping lists and English novels but hardly the approach we want to take with AIDS statistics or climatic data. One needn't be a positivist to believe that there are situations in which facts—and the correct interpretation of the facts—really matter. And indeed, facts matter a great deal in most areas of humanistic inquiry. It matters whether a work of art is by Rembrandt, as opposed to, say, Michelangelo or Lucian Freud. It certainly matters that the Treaty of Versailles was signed in 1919 (and not a year before or after). It seems to me absurd to act as if there were no practical difference between these kinds of claims and someone's political opinions or exegetical utterances. Surely, we can at least say that *fact* is a good word for those matters that aren't subject to widespread disagreement and debate (and to say so is neither to affirm nor reject correspondence theories of truth). Some humanists concern themselves with whether a particular painting is by Rembrandt, one of his students, or an art forger. Such scholars are looking for exactly this kind of fact and, in so doing, are quite literally trying to end disagreement and debate. When that happens, I assume they'll move on to something else. That someone might come along one day and question "the facts" (thus putting the subject back into the realm of debate) hardly reduces our need for some way to talk about what is known and what isn't (whatever one may ultimately decide about the philosophical nature of facts, truths, "states of affairs," and so forth).

But most humanistic problems don't look like this at all. The question isn't whether Rembrandt painted *The Night Watch* but why the girl just to the left of the captain receives the same amount of illumination as the captain. It's not that the armistice was signed in 1919 but the specific consequences of what John Maynard Keynes called the "Carthaginian Peace" imposed on Germany—a subject of much debate among historians and economists to this day. These discussions aren't quite freewheeling, but they're also not the sort of discussions that are easily settled by "agreement on the facts." If Rembrandt were to come back from the dead and say that *The Night Watch* is a forgery, we'd likely rejoice to have that bit of information (after we were done being astounded and more than slightly embarrassed). If Rembrandt were to come back from the dead and say that he meant nothing at all by the girl, we'd likely ignore him (just as we tend to do with Stoker).

Still, "In what ways does Bram Stoker's conflation of gender and politics reflect late-century anxieties?" is a question we pose not of the "data" but of the *text,* and asking whether the text—or something about language in general—constrains meaning in some way is a philosophical question with an exceedingly long history. When Hermogenes asks Socrates (who is late to the discussion) whether "there is a natural correctness of names," he is himself late to the discussion.[4] So is the (roughly contemporary) Sanskrit grammarian and philologist Pāṇini, who cites no less than ten linguists earlier than he who had probed the same questions. Yet despite the fact that most of the early progenitors of the linguistic turn in philosophy were themselves mathematicians concerned with questions in mathematical logic, very little of what we now call philosophy of language is concerned with *data* as we conventionally understand the term. Even the term *sense data* (introduced, it seems, by Bertrand Russell) has given way to the more ornate term *qualia.*

Perhaps this is only to say that "ordinary data" (by loose analogy with "ordinary language" in philosophy) is an undertheorized concept not only in the digital humanities but more broadly. Fisher's famous *Iris* data contain measurements of the parts of *Iris* flowers; such arrangement of signs and marks have not, generally speaking, prompted the strange propositions of analytical philosophy: Frege's "Everybody loves somebody,"[5] Russell's "The King of France is bald,"[6] Kaplan's "I am here now,"[7] or the ancient "This sentence is false." But even more pragmatic theories of language seem unable to overcome an entirely natural tendency among speakers of a language speaking about data. We may say that data involve the hidden and the manifest, cultural moves, weaponizations, and rhetorical persuasion. But are the numbers (and we can never seem to avoid the question) *right*? That would seem to suggest that somewhere, somehow, there is a nonnarrative substrate to data—that we can settle the facts and then interpret them. But even a laconic proposition like "The *Iris* dataset is wrong" is standing in for some other story: "The sepal lengths I recorded back in August are not the same as yours"; "You may have seen *Iris setosa* in the northern reaches of Canada, but it is *Iris kashmiriana* that adorns Muslim graves"; "These *Iris* are not Van Gogh's."

Data, in other words, becomes narrative so quickly that if an aporia were to appear that made narrative truly impossible, the proper term for the data would be *nonsense* in the strictest sense of the term—not analogous to a category error, or an "infelicitous sentence" (Chomsky's "colourless green ideas sleep furiously"), but something utterly un-recognizable as in any way implicated with language behavior.[8] We would not say, as we do when looking at tablets written in Linear A, that "we do not know what it means" but rather that we cannot use-fully imagine it meaning anything at all.[9] Wittgenstein famously de-clared that many (if not most) metaphysical propositions fall into this category, but his famous "refutation" of that argument—perhaps bet-ter thought of as a modulation—renders meaning the inevitable result of use and activity.[10] Lev Manovich was certainly wrong, therefore, to say that "narrative and database are natural enemies."[11] If anything, data and narrative are natural and inseparable allies. But even more wrongheaded are statements such as those made by Brian Vickers: "Abandoning the sequential interplay between words and treating them as separate items for computation destroys the possibility of *meaning.*"[12] The latter statement, in fact, is self-refuting.

It occurs in an article in the *Times Literary Supplement* that is meant to rebut the (admittedly extravagant) claims of Gary Taylor, who uses computational text analysis to argue that Shakespeare's cor-pus is rather more collaboratively authored than even partisans of this view (like Vickers) would ever admit. But while Vickers would like to imagine that venerable noncomputational methods ("study[ing] the text, looking for visible properties that might differentiate one dramatist from another" or "compar[ing] dramatists' phraseology") are naturally superior to the mathematical analysis of function words, he cannot avoid fighting data with more data (even when one lays aside the question of how "visible properties" and "phraseology" are somehow "not data").[13]

There's nothing wrong with trying to refute an argument that re-lies on data with more (or different) data, and there's certainly noth-ing wrong with suggesting that Gary Taylor is wrong. It might even make sense to make a casual distinction between "data-centric" argu-ments and arguments that do not repeatedly make reference to "what the data show" or "what the data mean." But it is certainly a category error to imagine that there is a thing called "human reading" (or some such) that is fully alive to nuance, contradiction, novelty, and the in-effable and then another kind of reading that, because it is focused on columns of numbers, words, frequencies, and properties, is incapable of such imaginative flights. That one may read data in such a way that only banality emerges is a fault of the analyst, not a logical consequence of something being designated as "data."

What's more, "data-centric argument" can only ever be a casual distinction, because it is difficult to imagine what a "dataless" narrative might look like. Vickers's own suspicions reflect a charge often made against text analysis (and, by association, against digital humanities):

> For many readers this is the fundamental weakness of quantitative attribution study, that it abandons meaning. The 100 or 500 words used most frequently by the target author(s) are reduced to mere items to be counted, without consideration of context or meaning. But many words have many meanings, which can only be construed by the context of use, and poets create unique contexts. Romeo's first words on seeing Juliet—"O she doth teach the torches to burn bright"—yields one word for the dataset, *torches.* Cleopatra's words on Antony's death—"The soldier's pole is fallen"—yields two, *soldier* and *pole.* In her mouth that is not just any pole but a metaphor for their intimacy.

I hope I have made the case that even a list as bare as "torches, soldier, pole" not only doesn't "abandon meaning" but actually can't do so (at least as long as humans are involved). But here, I'd like to ask why Vickers is so sure that Shakespeare's double entendre does not rise from an unacknowledged dataset. How, after all, does one know that *pole* is, in this instance, a phallic symbol? How would he defend that assertion to a group of skeptical students? He surely wouldn't offer a bare proposition: "Any time you encounter the word *pole,* it also means *penis.*" He would have to appeal instead to other instances of use, other contexts, other (invariably fragmentary) examples of language activity. He would have to, in other words, establish the claim by appealing to the "data."

It should be noted that arguments over matters like these often take a decidedly different turn. Digital humanists will immediately point out that metaphor detection is not something that necessarily lies beyond the ambit of computational analysis and that any hard-and-fast rules about what computers can and cannot do should be approached with caution. Fears of literary critics being replaced by robots soon follow, as the anxious titles of op-ed pieces amply demonstrate. "Technology Is Taking Over English Departments," says Adam Kirsch.[14] Timothy Brennan forecasts the "vast automation of teaching."[15] "Literature Is Not Data," says Stephen Marche, and the story of how the one became the other is a tale of "intellectual failure."[16] Lost in all of this are the startling philosophical implications of *how* a computer might go about detecting metaphors. "Metaphors are pervasive in natural language, and detecting them requires challenging contextual reasoning" is not a quote from Vickers or one of these broadsides but the first sentence in an article that shows how the use of bidirectional recurrent neural networks can successfully detect metaphors at an unprecedented level of accuracy (a claim they make without even glancing reference to once fashionable theories about the relationship between minds, brains, and computational neural networks).[17] In other words, the "quants" are very often making the same kinds of arguments that the "trads" summon to dismiss the activity.

This debate, though, is unfortunate, because the supposed hostility between data and narrative—between "columns of numbers" and the grand florilegia of expert interpretative discourse—is no mere canard. If data can never truly be separated from narrative and interpretation *for the same reasons* that meaning can never be separated from context, experience, embodiment, and subjectivity, then the nature of computational text analysis (and perhaps broad swaths of what we identify as digital humanities generally) becomes decidedly less radical. The entire debate, in fact, may properly belong to a different category of disputation.

In the latter half of the twentieth century, there emerged a fashion for period performances of Western classical music (in particular, of music written closer to the beginning of the so-called common practice period than the end). Hundreds of recordings were made using period instruments (which, in practice, meant instruments that were far less accurate and reliable than anything a modern musician would normally use). Musicologists reconsidered whether the customary tempos used in contemporary symphonic performances were historically accurate, argued over whether the configurations of modern orchestras were at all the same as they had been centuries earlier, and pored over contemporary accounts of those who had witnessed performances for clues. Modern ensembles responded with updated (or perhaps backdated) performances in accordance with these new discoveries. Audiences, by the 1980s, couldn't seem to get enough of these new interpretations, because (as concert programs and liner notes subtly implied) they were not interpretations at all. This, at last, was Beethoven's *Symphony No. 5* as it was meant to be heard. "Authentic performance" was, for a time, the term of art.

It is scarcely necessary to outline the general contours of the backlash that ensued. The most basic problem of all, of course, was whether the meager traces of historical evidence were enough to fully—or even partially—reconstruct a performance that left behind nothing more than a score that often, by modern standards, appears entirely fragmentary and elusive. Less charitable skeptics asked whether it might be necessary to dismantle the careful acoustic designs of modern concert halls, to turn off all air conditioning, open the windows to the din of horse-drawn carriages, or to have audiences stop bathing regularly in order to experience the proffered authenticity. Others provocatively insisted that the mania for authenticity was nothing more than a continuation of the modernist impulse:

> What we had been accustomed to regard as historically authentic performances, I began to see, represented neither any determinable historical prototype nor any coherent revival of practices coeval with the repertories they addressed. Rather, they embodied a whole wish list of modern(ist) values, validated in the academy and the marketplace alike by an eclectic, opportunistic reading of historical evidence.[18]

At base, though, the mania for authentic performance (now more likely to bear the far less provocative title "historically informed performance") was about methodology. The question became—or, rather, was revealed to have always been—the question of *what* we are interpreting. It had seemed obvious to Aaron Copland (writing in 1957) that instrumentalists and conductors (and, finally, listeners) were *interpreting* a score written by a composer.[19] The period performance revival sought to ask whether the score written by a composer was the only thing about music that was subject to interpretation.

There were (and are) many reasons to rejoice over this turn of events. Composers whose work had been neglected suddenly reappeared, and parts of the standard repertory now emerged in sometimes shockingly new formations. No one doubts that the study of the historical circumstances in which a piece of music was written and performed deepens our understanding of that music (even if an interpreter chooses to ignore those circumstances), and this methodological principle is hardly confined to music. It is not merely an interesting side note that *The Pickwick Papers* appeared in serial form over the course of nineteen months, that it may have begun with a request that the author provide descriptions for a series of comic illustrations, or that the novel (?) inspired a group of clubs and societies. One is perfectly free to find period performances dull and uninspiring or to think it more useful to read Dickens neatly bound in paperback. It may well be that a sudden obsession with the context of the past says much more about who we are than who anyone might have been. But two particular objections seem to me to be actively hostile to the project of interpretation.

The first is to say that shifting and expanding the locus of interpretation is, by nature, an epistemologically flawed maneuver. That might seem an extreme position, but it is precisely what is alleged when critics say that "literature is not data" or that historical musicology has no bearing on interpretation. Many are surely within their rights to declare "computational literary criticism" (or period performances) to be at odds with other (presumably better) goals. But it is only from the exaggerated epistemology in which changing the terms of interpretation itself is forbidden that baldly absurd forecasts of the death of English studies and robot conductor uprisings emerge. This is an entirely vital distinction. Absurdities do not necessarily follow from the statement that the Bible can be interpreted allegorically; absurdities follow inevitably from the belief that it *cannot* be interpreted this way.

The second—far more common among partisans than detractors—is the belief that shifting and expanding the locus of interpretation leads not merely to a more expansive interpretative affordance but to a singular affordance that must perforce replace all others. There were undoubtedly musicologists who felt that everything heretofore had been wrong and others who felt they had discovered not only the truth of the past but, by extension (echoing Schoenberg's plangent confidence), the truth of the future. There is something of this in the strange logic of Moretti's enthusiasm for distant reading:

> I began this chapter by saying that quantitative data are useful because they are independent of interpretation; then, that they are challenging because they often demand an interpretation that transcends the quantitative realm; now, most radically, we see them falsify existing theoretical explanations.[20]

Moretti would undoubtedly demure were I to charge him with advancing an untenable philosophical exclusivity, but the seeds are sown in passages such as this: that which is initially advanced as merely useful becomes transcendent—radically (and uniquely) separating truth from falsehood.

Perhaps this is an inevitable temptation. In the end, one would like to be right about something in the gauzy and uncertain world of literary hermeneutics, and not just about quotidian matters (at least once in a while). That "reducing texts to data" cannot provide this certainty may even strike some partisans as disappointing. But in the end, discovering that data (at least of the sort that interests humanists) are just other kinds of text, just other objects for discussion, yet more occasion for narrative, might be reassuring, if not liberating. That we cannot so easily break out of humanistic methods of inquiry (while still engaging in humanistic discussion) suggests that the discussion, in all its variegated splendor, does possess some kind of unity that distinguishes it from other forms of discourse. If that unity ends up being a refusal (and not, as Gadamer once wrote, merely a "lack") of methodological boundaries, we can be certain that our datasets are as inexhaustible as any other object we draw into view.

How to Do Things (to Texts) with Computers

Early on in my teaching career—while I was still in graduate school—a student in one of my Shakespeare classes came up to ask me a question that puzzled me. I had just got done explaining to the class that I wanted them to write a critical essay on a Shakespeare play. I told them how long it should be, that it had to be double-spaced, listed some sources they might look at, and told them that in my infinite largesse, I had set the due date so that they wouldn't have to trouble themselves about it over spring break. I thought I had been quite clear about the requirements, but one student came up to me afterward looking very distraught. "I don't understand! What are we supposed to *do*?"

Now, I was a quite inexperienced teacher at the time, but nonetheless, you might suppose that I had a snappy answer. I had written lots of critical essays at that point; surely I could explain how to do it in a way that goes beyond the bare matter of how to set the line spacing correctly. But instead, I stammered something along the lines of, "You know, write an essay about Shakespeare!" and moved on to my next class.

I wasn't happy with that answer, of course, and I still cringe a bit when I think about it. I knew that I had failed to take advantage of a "teaching moment," as they say. But even assuming a beautifully rendered essay prompt, the question still stands: What is it, exactly, that we are asking our students to do when we tell them to write a critical essay or give "a reading" of a work of literature? What is it that *I'm* doing when *I* do these things (another thing I should presumably know about)?

The question, to put it another way, was a lot smarter than my answer. To begin with, this student was asking a perfectly legitimate question. Whatever a critical reading is, it seems qualitatively different from plain-old reading—the sort of thing you do on the beach or before drifting off to sleep at night. But the language that surrounds that discourse ("Did you like it?" "What's it about?") is more or less forbidden in literary-critical discourse. If you want to do poorly in an English class, all you have to do is either engage in aesthetic rapture or recapitulate the plot. It's not that these are bad ways to talk about books, or even unsophisticated ways; if anything, they represent the natural ways. But the critical mode is different, and we're not born knowing how to do it.

My answer, moreover, was deeply misleading. The student had asked what she was supposed to *do* with the text; I answered that she was supposed to do something *about* the text. The question, in fact, had struck upon the Greek root of the word *drama*—δράω: to do, or act—which seems a more appropriate way to talk about critical engagement (particularly with dramatic works). I had made it sound as if I wanted this person to make an arrest ("you better do something about that Shakespeare character!").

I did eventually come up with a way to explain what I want my students to do, and I've been giving some version of this sermon for the last twenty years. It goes like this: study the play (or the novel, or the poem, or whatever it is) until you see some nonobvious pattern, and then explain to me (or to your reader) why I should see that pattern as well. This is more complicated than it sounds, and certainly harder, but ultimately, it's a practical definition. "I liked it" isn't a pattern. The plot *is* a pattern, but the bare "facts" of the plot are obvious. Critical reading doesn't explain what happened in *The Comedy of Errors* but instead tries to show us that, for example, all the mistaken identities in the play (the pattern of identity, if you like) reveal the work to be both a modification of the traditional terms of Plautine farce and a commentary on the emergence of a distinct vision of the self in the early modern period. If anyone can already see this plainly, it probably fails the nonobvious test (it would, at this point, for just about any Shakespeare scholar, though once upon a time it might not have—a matter of indifference in an undergraduate course). If I can't convince you that it is important to see what I see, then I'm probably not actually arguing a position. Maybe I'm paraphrasing (the deadliest trap for beginners, and one of the hardest to overcome); maybe I haven't fully thought out where this "pattern" actually leads. Maybe I haven't convinced myself that it's all that important.

Such maneuvers are not, of course, limited to literary criticism. Pattern and explanation inform the rhetoric of humanistic inquiry in all its forms. The historian doesn't tell us *that* Napoleon lost the battle of Waterloo but that he lost it because the Duke of Wellington was a talented coalition general who was able to create more robust communication lines across wider distances than his opponent. The art critic, likewise, doesn't simply enumerate the philosophers represented in Raphael's *School of Athens* but shows us how the various groupings reflect early modern visions of the organization of knowledge. Philosophy, at least in its more strongly analytical forms, might exploit the power of pattern more fully than any other humanistic discipline. Even the earliest breathings of syllogistic logic were not, in the end, about what was being argued but about whether there was something about the pattern of argumentation that justified (or falsified) a particular set of inferences. The primacy of pattern also helps to explain why many believe that mathematics should be considered a humanities discipline, as it was in previous centuries. Few definitions, I think, capture its essence as well as the one offered by the mathematician Keith Devlin: "Mathematics is *the science of patterns*."[1]

I relate this story, and advance the (admittedly loose) methodological framework that eventually followed from it, because I believe it explains why that branch of digital humanities concerned with literary criticism and text analysis has largely failed to penetrate the mainstream of scholarly discourse in the humanities. In explaining itself—and indeed, in carrying out its own methodological project—it has put forth the same weak answer I gave to my student years ago. Against the hermeneutical injunction to do something with the text—discover patterns we might form into critical explanations—it has instead chosen to do something *about* the text.

The trend began early. John Burrows and Hugh Craig, in their groundbreaking work on Romantic and Renaissance drama, believe the chief point to be drawn from their scatter plots and correlation matrices is that none of what they found contradicted the findings of earlier critics.[2] Louis Milic believed that "the low frequency of initial determiners, taken together with the high frequency of initial connectives, made [Jonathan Swift] a writer who likes transitions and made much of connectives."[3] Susan Hockey appears to offer such tautologies as among the principal virtues of computer-assisted work: "The computer is best at finding features or patterns within a literary work and counting occurrences of those features."[4]

It is difficult not to read, in these refusals to engage fully with the hermeneutical process of pattern formation and explication, a subtle, inchoate desire to assuage fears of a mechanized literary criticism or, alternatively, a machinic instantiation of Wordsworth's famous quip: a dissection that amounts to a murder. Such fears, of course, go back (like computing in the humanities) to the days of punch card machines, when many of the anxieties concerning computers and automation were cathected onto the punch card itself: "Do not fold, spindle, or mutilate."[5] Yet folding, spindling, and mutilating are at once the basis of computation (which nearly always produces an alternate arrangement of the data) and the means by which we come to locate the patterns upon which reading depends. Why, then, this refusal to let computers lead us fully—without apology and without tentativeness—into interpretation and explanation? Let's put that differently: What would computer technology, with its apparent disposition toward unerring processes and irrefragable answers, look like if it were loosed from the strictures of the irrefragable and allowed to become a bionic extension of our ability to deduce patterns and a launching pad for our bold attempts to explain those patterns? I believe we would have something that looks a lot less like the digital humanities' ironic alignment with experimental science and a lot more like the implicitly humanistic methods of mathematics. An example will help to illustrate what I mean.

In 1741, the great Swiss mathematician Leonhard Euler (1707–1783) proposed a solution to what has come be known as the bridges of Königsberg problem. Königsberg, a small Prussian town during the eighteenth century, was divided into four sections (including one island) by the river Pregolya.[6] The four regions were connected to one another by seven bridges, and the townspeople, who were fond of taking walks about the city on Sunday afternoons, wondered if it was possible to wander about the town crossing each bridge only once and ending up back where you started (see Figure 6).

The problem, it turns out, is not as easy as it looks—particularly if you want to *prove* that there is (or is not) a way to cross the bridges

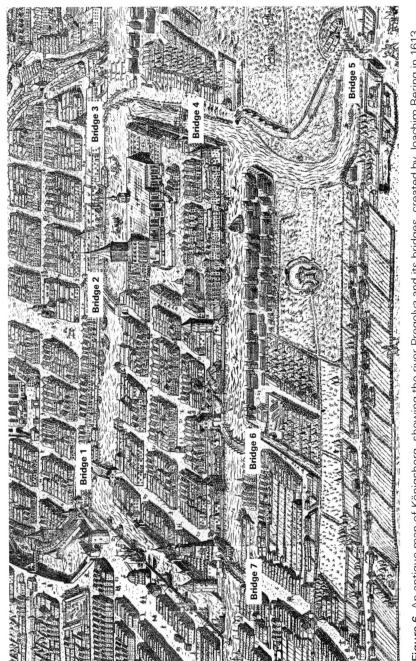

Figure 6. An antique map of Königsberg, showing the river Pregolya and its bridges, created by Joachim Bering in 1613.

this way. The essay in which Euler proposes his solution is not only one of the founding works of both topology and graph theory but a masterpiece of mathematical exposition for the deftness with which Euler dismisses brute-force solutions in favor of more subtle mathematical observations.[7]

Euler begins by creating a simple schematic diagram of the regions that the river divides (Figure 7); a modern graph theorist, in an attempt to remove all interference from the space of the problem, might collapse the regions and crossings into points and lines (Figure 8).

Such representations of the data constitute one of the basic means by which we arrive at meaning—in literary criticism as surely as in mathematics. By distilling the problem down, Euler is able to see that the problem of the Königsberg bridges may be envisioned as a

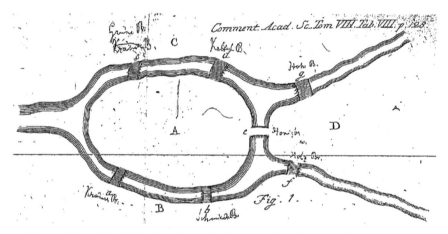

Figure 7. Leonhard Euler's schematic drawing of the bridges of Königsberg, originally published in *Solutio problematis ad geometriam situs pertinentis.*

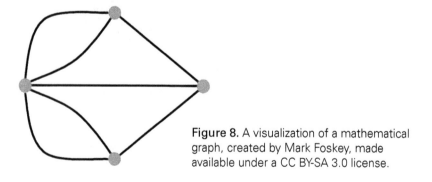

Figure 8. A visualization of a mathematical graph, created by Mark Foskey, made available under a CC BY-SA 3.0 license.

problem not of the bridges but of the land masses that they connect. With his vision trained on the land masses, Euler discerns the obvious fact that in order for someone to trace a continuous line through every point (without crossing over the same line more than once), every point would have to have a line leading toward it and a different line leading away from it—or, if there is more than one way onto the land, several pairs of such lines. The starting and end points may be an exception to this, but even in this case, the graph could only have (at most) two points with an odd number of lines leading away from them.[8] The graph makes it clear that this is not the case with the bridges of Königsberg. The proposed journey is impossible. This result is further generalizable and is one of the basic theorems of graph theory: a connected multigraph has a Euler circuit if and only if each of its vertices has an even degree.

Euler's solution is an elegant one; despite the difficulty of the problem, once it is seen in a certain light (a certain arrangement), it strikes us with the force of the obvious and thus obviates the need for a prohibitively exhaustive brute-force search through possible solutions. The real interest of Euler's solution for our purposes, however, lies in the fact that his method moved from one arrangement to another until a pattern enabled the insight necessary for a solution—an insight that was difficult for the pedestrian (or even the map reader) to see. The pattern itself is not the solution. It is instead the means by which Euler leads himself to the most useful interpretation of the problem.

In conceiving of the relationship between computers and humanistic study, it may be disingenuous to ask how we can create programs that can do literary criticism, philosophy, or historical analysis—not because we lack the elusive "strong AI" these tasks would presumably require but because the question presupposes that doing these things is entirely a matter of interpretation. Interpretation is, to be sure, the sine qua non of humanistic inquiry, but it is only part of the process (and, we might say, a latter part). The other part is more serendipitous and ludic—closer to the following of a hunch or the formulation of a strategy. One wonders how much time Euler spent tracing his finger over the map of Königsberg, trying this pattern and then that one, looking for something that would lead to the crucial moment of vision. We long for a machine that can give us the hermeneutical equivalent of the Euler circuit, but perhaps our efforts would be better directed toward creating a machine that can help us doodle. In other words, a machine that can assist at the moment when critical engagement leads to critical insight.

How, then, does one doodle with a Shakespeare play?

It is customary, in interpreting Shakespeare's *Antony and Cleopatra,* to think of Alexandria in terms of license, nature, and femininity and Rome in terms of stoicism, stability, and masculinity. With this binary overlay in place, many have come to regard the play as a political and erotic negotiation between two worlds personified by the Egyptian characters, on the one hand, and the Roman characters, on the other. It is a useful pattern, which has facilitated countless classroom discussions and yielded hundreds of critical articles.[9]

But what if we wrote a program that could automatically do to a Shakespeare play what Euler did to Königsberg (see Figure 9)?[10] We arrive at something quite different from the obligatory maps of the ancient world that often accompany editions of this play. Like Harry Beck's ingenious and widely imitated map of the London Tube, this "map" regards physical distance and direction as irrelevant. The lines in the graph (each of which is labeled with the appropriate act and scene numbers) represent the passage in the space of the drama from one location to the next, but the locations are more abstract. Scene locations that have more adjacent edges than others are said to be (in graph theoretical terms) vertexes of higher degree. Alexandria and Rome have, predictably, the highest degrees (with Alexandria displaying the highest number of adjacent scenes). Cleopatra's monument, which is both the last scene of the play and the only scene that takes place in that location, is a "pendant node" or vertex of degree one.

To read *Antony and Cleopatra* is to be aware that Rome and Alexandria are not the only settings in which the action occurs, but it is difficult to appreciate the range of locations in which the play occurs (Sicily, Misenum, Syria, Athens, Actium, Taenarum, and several places in and around Alexandria) and to perceive the amount of stage action they take up. The graph, by contrast, allows us not only to see the relationships among these other scenes more clearly but to perceive them in terms of the play's general movement "between" Rome and Alexandria. Three scenes lead toward Rome (Sicily, Misenum, and Syria) and several away from Rome (Actium, Taenarum, Caesar's Camp, and an indeterminate battlefield). This, of course, does not correspond precisely to the chronology of the play, which, for

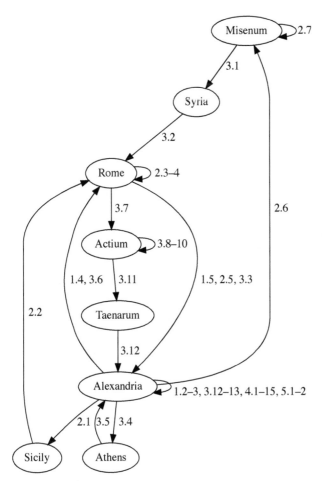

Figure 9. The scene changes in Shakespeare's *Antony and Cleopatra* represented as a directed, acyclic graph. Created by the author. Image made available under a CC BY-SA 4.0 license.

the reader, stands as the dominant organizing structure. There is, for example, no central Roman scene dividing the early events of the play from the Battle of Actium in the latter half of Act 3. The scene set in Sicily (2.1) passes to three subsequent scenes in Rome (2.2–4), but from there back to Alexandria (2.5) before passing through Misenum (2.6–7) and Syria (3.1) on the way to Rome again (3.2).

The division of the play into scenes is, of course, the product of centuries of pattern recognition beginning with Nicholas Rowe's 1709 edition of the play; the 1623 Folio has neither act nor scene division, nor even indications of setting. The play, in other words, comes to us as something already "patterned" by centuries of reading and commentary. In our case, the divisions have a purpose even more efficacious than what is required by the exigencies of reading or performance, since they constitute the data points of a representation that illustrates other patterns.

All of the scenes to which the graph draws our attention are sites of confusion and uncertainty among the characters and serendipitous changes in the action. Scenes from the earlier movement toward Rome are heavily laden with dramatic irony—a device used infrequently in this play but significantly in these scenes and in Cleopatra's message to Antony reporting her death in 4.14. As 2.1 begins, Pompey is in Sicily making plans for war based on the knowledge that Antony remains in Egypt when Varrius reports as "most certain" the fact that "Mark Antony is every hour in Rome / expected" (ll. 28–31).[11] Scene 2.6 begins in Misenum with the certainty of war but ends with the promise of a celebrated peace. Scene 2.7 celebrates the agreement between Pompey and the triumvirate (not on the hill of Misenum but displaced farther "between" in a galley at sea). Throughout that scene we are given knowledge of various disjunctions between the actual and the apparent. All seems convivial, but we come to find out that Menas is plotting the murder of the triumvirate. Lepidus believes he is learning about the nature of crocodiles, when in fact he is merely hearing tautologies ("It is shaped, sir, like itself, and it is as broad as it hath breadth," ll. 42–43). Pompey believes he has the loyalty of Menas, but the latter reveals to us in an aside his intention to "never follow thy palled fortunes more" (l. 82).

The scenes corresponding to the nodes leading away from Rome, by contrast, emphasize the characters' full awareness of realities alternative to the apparent ones. No sooner has the triumvirate celebrated their renewed union than we are taken to Sicily where Ventidius, having just avenged the death of Marcus Crassus, reminds us of the fragility of the first triumvirate (3.1). In Athens, Octavia becomes aware of the impossibility of stable relations: "A more unhappy lady, / If this division chance, ne'er stood between, / Praying for both parts . . . no midway / 'Twixt these extremes at all" (3.4.12–14, 18–19). Having chosen to engage Caesar on the indeterminate and insubstantial sea at Actium, Antony reverses course and leaves Enobarbus dumbfounded.

> SCARUS: On our side, like the tokened pestilence
> Where death is sure. Yon ribaudred nag of Egypt—

Whom leprosy o'ertake—i'th' midst o'th' fight
when vantage like a pair of twins appeared
Both as the same—or, rather, ours the elder—
The breeze upon her, like a cow in June,
Hoists sails and flies.
ENOBARBUS: That I beheld.
Mine eyes did sicken at the sight and could not
Endure a further view.
SCARUS: She once being loofed,
The noble ruin of her magic, Antony,
Claps on his sea-wing and,—like a doting mallard—
Leaving the flight in height, flies after her!
I never saw an action of such shame.
Experience, manhood, honor ne'er before
Did violate so itself. (3.10.9–24)

The scene in which Antony is most reduced and dissipated by defeat—
"unqualitied with very shame" (3.11.44)—significantly occurs in an
unspecified location.

To the oppositions of masculinity and femininity, nature and civilization, stoicism and license, we may therefore add the opposition of
apparent reality to the transformative power of that tragic vision that
perceives the contingency of reality.[12] This latter opposition serves to
locate this apparently heterodox tragedy in the same general pattern
of *Hamlet, King Lear,* and *Othello,* where the world at first appears
to the protagonists as governed by a set of inviolate laws: daughters
love their fathers, wives love their husbands, subjects obey their
king, murders are always avenged. The tragedy is set in motion by the
knowledge that the world might be otherwise—an inexorable telos
that exacts vision and knowledge at the price of freedom.

Each character necessarily inscribes a path that constitutes at least
one subgraph of the overall topology of the drama. In order to capture this movement, we can ask the computer to analyze the graphs
in terms of which characters appear in which locations and how they
move in and out of the "geography" of the play. When we do this with
Antony, we discover that his movement ranges over nearly every location in the play.

Cleopatra's path, by contrast, is confined to Egypt and Actium. But
conceiving of these appearances specifically as movements through

interlocking spaces draws our attention to a singularity that is hard to see in the text: Antony and Cleopatra share not only Alexandria but the two liminal locations moving *away* from Rome and, besides these, another uncertain location "outside Alexandria." It is here that Antony briefly retreats for a better view ("Where yond pine does stand / I shall discover all," 4.12.1–2) and where he witnesses his own men going over to Caesar's army. He then accuses Cleopatra of betrayal; she appears but offers no response.

Where do we go with this? How about here: *Antony and Cleopatra* has long been understood as a play that contrasts the license and femininity of Alexandria with the stoic masculinity of Rome. But this is not merely a matter of contrast. The play negotiates these two realms in terms of a set of locations between and on the margins of either place and, in fact, presents the tragic turning point as having occurred precisely "no place." The knowledge that precipitates the tragic awareness of fragility and contingency is therefore located not merely in the psyche of the main characters (who are neither driven to madness nor paralyzed by inaction—the typical pattern in the major tragedies) but within extended metaphors of land and territory. One of the ways in which *Antony and Cleopatra* succeeds in becoming both a history play and a tragedy is by constructing "a place between"—a version, and perhaps an evolution, of Lear's moor and Macbeth's heath—that serves to concretize tragic vision as something already built into the rise and fall of empires.

It would be an absurdity to maintain that the graph that led me to the insight is itself an interpretation of the play (at least in the same way that the reading of the graph is) or that it somehow "proves" that the reading is correct. The maneuvers that the program provokes simply reframe the play's intelligibility by creating alternative textual and graphical arrangements. Yet such rearrangements are nonetheless essential to the project of interpretation.

An objection presents itself. The processes of pattern formation that the graphing program performs could surely have been undertaken with pencil and paper, the computer merely adding speed (and perhaps a bit of showiness) to the process. The first half of this objection is accurate as far as it goes, though it might be noted that virtually any computational process can, at least in principle, be undertaken with pencil and paper. Adding twenty-digit numbers, preparing manuscripts, and drawing diagrams were all done with the simplest of writing instruments for centuries before the advent of computers. Even extremely difficult applications, such as predicting the weather from simulative models, are not technically beyond the ambit of paper and brush. There is no inherent connection between the electro-mechanical device we call a computer and the formal abstraction we call an algorithm. Donald Knuth, author of the monumental *Art of Computer Programming,* considers it fundamental to the definition of an algorithm that "its operations must all be sufficiently basic that they can in principle be done exactly and in a finite amount of time by someone using pencil and paper."[13] Even the most enthusiastic partisans of computer technology will have to concede that in the end, it all comes down to speed and automation.

It would be a grave mistake, however, to minimize the significance of speed and automation either as cultural commodities or as philosophical categories. N. Katherine Hayles, echoing McLuhan, notes that speed of access is the defining feature of such systems:

> Confronted with the theory and practice of hypertextuality, many people insist that it is nothing new. After all, they say, *Paradise Lost* was published in print books with appendices and footnotes long before hypertext appeared on the scene. Nothing has changed with the hypertext version, these people argue, except speed of access. But for human memory, speed of access is crucial. It often makes the difference in whether self-organizing processes spontaneously emerge or not. A recondite reader may of course do for herself what the naive reader does when he repeats the sentence— mentally rehearse the footnote on page 497 while looking at the text on page 216 so that both are held in short-term memory together. This takes effort, however, and most readers will make it only occasionally if at all. By facilitating these juxtapositions, and especially by shortening the time it takes to make them, hypertext encourages self-organization.[14]

Similar claims for the transformative power of speed could be made in numerous contexts. Satellite communications, email, television, and the web have not merely added speed to the capable messenger on horseback. Our sense of the world has been radically altered by the automation of the slower systems.

Automation, which is often both the cause and the effect of speed, moves the task that a particular algorithm performs out of the realm of the problem space. Elementary schoolchildren are today capable of algorithmic calculations (such as long division) that left entire ancient civilizations baffled. They do this by employing "automatic" algorithms, which, because they are fast and performed with a minimum of effort, allow the student to focus on some more interesting problem. Because the graphing program produces graphs almost instantaneously and may be trained on any play without much trouble, we are able to use it to study aspects of Shakespearean drama that might simply have been too laborious to construct by hand.

Of course, someone (namely, me) had to figure out how to get a computer to represent a Shakespeare play as a graph. The solution is neither as elegant nor as useful as long division, which required a truly sublime act of human ingenuity to devise. But if digital humanities were to focus on facilitating the process of pattern formation—which is another way of referring to the process of critical engagement—it might one day produce something as transparently beautiful. Such a tool might be to humanistic study what the telescope or the particle accelerator is to science—not simply a study aid but a means by which the field of inquiry itself is expanded and new interpretive valences unleashed. Who knows what we could do then?

The Hermeneutics of
Screwing Around

According to the World Wide Web, the phrase "So many books, so little time" originates with Frank Zappa. I don't believe it, myself. If I had to guess, I would have said maybe Erasmus or Trithemius. But even if I'm right, I'm probably wrong. This is one of civilization's oldest laments—one that, in spirit, predates the book itself. There has never been a time when philosophers—lovers of wisdom, broadly understood—have not exhibited profound regret over the impedance mismatch between time and truth. For surely, there are more books, more ideas, more experiences, and more relationships worth having than there are hours in a day (or days in a lifetime).

What everyone wants—what everyone from Sargon to Zappa has wanted—is some coherent, authoritative path through what is known. That's the idea behind *Dr. Eliot's Five-Foot Shelf of Books,* Adler's *Great Books of the Western World,* Modern Library's 100 Best Books, and all other similar attempts to condense knowledge into some ordered list of things the educated should know. It's also the idea behind every syllabus, every curriculum, and most of the non-fiction books that have ever been written. The world is vast. Art is long. What else can we do but survey the field, introduce a topic, plant a seed (with, what else, a seminar). Amazon has a feature that allows users to create reading guides focused on a particular topic. They call it, appropriately, "Listmania."

While the anxiety of not knowing the path is constant, moments of cultural modernity provide especially fertile ground for the creation of epitomes, summae, canons, and bibles (as well as new schools, new curricula, and new ways of organizing knowledge). It is, after all, at the end of history that one undertakes summation of "the best that has been thought and said in the world."[1] The aforementioned great books lists all belong to the early decades of the twentieth century, when U.S. cultural anxiety—especially concerning its relationship to Europe—could be leavened with a bold act of cultural confidence. Thomas Jefferson had said something similar at a time closer to the founding of the country when he noted, "All that is necessary for a student is access to a library, and directions in what order the books are to be read."[2] But the same phenomenon—the same play of anxiety and confidence—was at work in the writing of the Torah, the *Summa*, Will and Ariel Durant's *Story of Civilization,* and all efforts of similar grandeur. All three of those works were written not just during moments of rapid cultural change but during periods of anxiety about change. "These words YHWH spoke to your entire assembly at the mountain from the midst of the fire, the cloud, and the fog (with) a great voice, adding no more" (Deut. 5:19);[3] "We purpose in this book to treat of whatever belongs to the Christian religion, in such a way as may tend to the instruction of beginners";[4] "I wish to tell as much as I can, in as little space as I can, of the contributions that genius and labor have made to the cultural heritage of mankind."[5] This essay will not aim quite so high.

Even in the very early days of the web, one felt the soul-crushing lack of order. One of the first pages I ever visited was "Jerry and David's Guide to the World Wide Web," which endeavored to, what else, guide you through what seemed an already impossibly vast expanse of information.[6] Google might seem something else entirely, but it shares the basic premise of those quaint guides of yore, and of all guides to knowledge. The point is not to return the over three million pages that relate in some way to Frank Zappa. The point is to say, "Relax. Here is where you start. Look at this. Then look at this."

We might say that all such systems rely on an act of faith, but it's not so much trust in the search engine (or the book, or the professor) as it is willingness to suspend disbelief about the yellow wood after having taken a particular road. Literary historian Franco Moretti states the situation starkly:

> We've just started rediscovering what Margaret Cohen calls the "great unread." "I work on West European narrative, etc. . . ." Not really, I work on its canonical fraction, which is not even one per cent of published literature. And again, some people

have read more, but the point is that there are thirty thousand nineteenth-century British novels out there, forty, fifty, sixty thousand—no one really knows, no one has read them, no one ever will. And then there are French novels, Chinese, Argentinian, American ...[7]

Debates about canonicity have been raging in my field (literary studies) for as long as the field has been around. Who's in? Who's out? How do we decide? Moretti reminds us of the dispiriting fact that this problem has no practical solution. It's not just that someone or something will be left off; it's that our most inclusive, most enlightened choices will fail against even the most generous requirements for statistical significance. The syllabus represents the merest fraction of the professor's knowledge, and the professor's knowledge is, in the scheme of things, embarrassingly slight.

Greg Crane, who held a series of symposia on the general question "What Do You Do with a Million Books?" a few years ago, rightly identifies it as an ancient calculus:

The Greek historian Herodotus has the Athenian sage Solon estimate the lifetime of a human being at c. 26,250 days (Herodotus, *The Histories*, 1.32). If we could read a book on each of those days, it would take almost forty lifetimes to work through every volume in a single million book library. The continuous tradition of written European literature that began with the Iliad and Odyssey in the eighth century BCE is itself little more than a million days old. While libraries that contain more than one million items are not unusual, print libraries never possessed a million books of use to any one reader.[8]

Way too many books, way too little time.

But again, the real anxiety is not that the Library of Congress contains over five hundred human lifetimes worth of reading material (I'm using the highly generous Solon-Crane metric, which assumes you read a book every day from the day you're born until the day you die). The problem is that that much information probably exceeds our ability to create reliable guides to it. It's one thing to worry that your canon isn't sufficiently inclusive, or broad, or representative. It's another thing when your canon has no better chance of being these things than a random selection. When we get up into the fourteen-million-book range, books that are known by more than two living people are already "popular." A book like *Hamlet* has overcome enormous mathematical odds that ruthlessly favor obscurity; the fact that millions of people have read it might become a compelling argument for why you should read it too. But in the end, arguments from the standpoint of popularity satisfy neither the canoniclast nor the historian. The dark fear is that no one can really say what is "representative," because no one has any basis for making such a claim.

Several solutions have been proposed, including proud ownership of our ignorance and dilettantism. A few years ago, Pierre Bayard famously—and with only the barest sheen of satire—exposed our condition by writing a book entitled *How to Talk about Books You Haven't Read*. In it, intellectual facility is presented as a kind of trick: "For knowing how to speak with finesse about something with which we are unacquainted has value far beyond the realm of books."[9] It is a lesson thoroughly absorbed by anyone who stands on the right side of a PhD oral exam. But amazingly, even Bayard sees this as a means toward guiding people through knowledge:

> [Students] see culture as a huge wall, as a terrifying specter of "knowledge." But we intellectuals, who are avid readers, know there are many ways of reading a book. You can skim it, you can start and not finish it, you can look at the index. You learn to live with a book. . . . I want to help people organize their own paths through culture.[10]

At some level, there is no difference at all between Pierre Bayard and, say, Mortimer Adler. Both believe in culture. Both believe that one can find an ordered path through culture. Bayard just thinks there are faster ways to do it than starting with volume 1 of *Great Books of the Western World*. Indeed, Adler himself almost seems to agree; books two and three of *Great Books* present what he calls a "Synopticon." What could such a thing be but the CliffsNotes to the main ideas of Western civilization? There also isn't much of a difference between Bayard, on the one hand, and Crane and Moretti, on the other. All three would like us to dispense with the silly notion that we can read everything, so that we can get on with the task of organizing our own paths through culture. It is true that the latter—as well as digital humanists generally—propose that we use computers, but I would like to argue that that difference is not as crucial as it seems.

There have always been two ways to deal with a library. The first is the one we're most used to thinking about. I am doing research on the influence of French composer Edgard Varèse on the early work of Frank Zappa. I go to the library and conduct an investigation, which might include the catalog, a bibliography or two, the good people at the reference desk, or any one of a dozen different methods and tools. This is search. I know what I'm looking for, and I have various strategies for locating it. I can't read everything on this subject. I can't even locate everything on this subject. But I have faith in the idea that I can walk out of the library (this afternoon, or after ten years of focused research, depending on my situation) being able to speak intelligently and convincingly on this topic.

The second way goes like this: I walk into the library and wander around in a state of insouciant boredom. I like music, so I head over to the music section. I pick up a book on American rock music and start flipping through it (because it's purple and big). There's an interesting bit on Frank Zappa, and it mentions that Zappa was way into this guy named Edgard Varèse. I have no idea who that is, so I start looking around for some Varèse. One look at the cover of his biography—Varèse with that mad-scientist look and the wild hair—and I'm already a fan. And so off I go. I check out some records and discover Varèse.

This is called browsing, and it's a completely different activity. Here, I don't know what I'm looking for, really. I just have a bundle of interests and proclivities. I'm not really trying to find "a path through culture." I'm really just screwing around. This is more or less how Zappa discovered Varèse. He had read an article in *Look* magazine in which the owner of the Sam Goody record chain was bragging about his ability to sell obscure records like *The Complete Works of Edgard Varèse, Vol. 1*.[11] The article describes Varèse's music as "a weird jumble of drums and other unpleasant sounds."[12] The rest is history (of the sort that you can search for, if you're so inclined).

We think of the computer as a device that has revolutionized search—*information retrieval,* to use the formal term—and that is of course true. Until recently, no one was able to search the content of all the books in the library. There was no way to ask, "Which of these books contains the phrase *Frank Zappa*?" The fact that we can now do that changes everything, but it doesn't change the nature of the thing. When we ask that question—or any question, for that matter—we are still searching. We are still asking a question and availing ourselves of various technologies in pursuit of the answer.

Browsing, though, is a different matter. Once you have programmatic access to the content of the library, screwing around potentially becomes a far more illuminating and useful activity. That is, presumably, why we call the navigational framework one uses to poke around the World Wide Web a "browser," as opposed to, say, a "searcher." From the very start, the web outstripped our ability to say what is actually there. Jerry and David couldn't say it then and Google can't say it even now. "Can I help you?" "No, I'm just browsing." Translation: "I just got here! How can you help me find what I'm looking for when (a) I don't know what's here and (b) I don't know what I'm looking for?" The salesclerk, of course, doesn't need a translation. He or she understands perfectly that you're just screwing around. Our irritation arises not because the question is premature or impertinent but because we're being encouraged to have a purposive experience when we're perfectly happy having a serendipitous one.

And that is absolutely not what the people who are thinking about the brave new world of large-scale digital corpora (Google Books, or the web itself) want to talk about. Consider Martin Mueller's notion of "not reading"—an idea he puts forth during a consideration of the power of the digital surrogate:

> A book sits in a network of transactions that involve a reader, his interlocutors, and a "collective library" of things one knows or is supposed to know. Felicitous reading—I adapt the term from John Austin's definition of felicitous speech acts—is the art of locating with sufficient precision the place a given book occupies in that network at a given moment. Your skill as a reader, then, is measured by the speed and accuracy with which you can do that. Ideally you should do it in "no time at all." Once you have oriented a book in the right place of its network, you can stop reading. In fact, you should stop reading.[13]

Perhaps this isn't "search," classically understood, but it's about as far from screwing around as the average game theory symposium is from poker night. You go to the archive to set things right—to increase the likelihood that your network of associations corresponds to the actual one (or, as seems more likely, the culturally dominant one). That technology could assist you in this august task—the task of a lifetime, for most of us—should not obscure the fundamental conservatism of this vision. The vast digital library is there to help you answer the question with which you began.

Greg Crane imagines a library in which the books talk to each other—each one embedded in a swirl of data mining and machine learning algorithms. What do we do with a million books? His answer is boldly visionary: "Extract from the stored record of humanity useful information in an actionable format for any given human being of any culture at any time and in any place."[14] He notes that this "will not emerge quickly," but one might legitimately question whether, strictly speaking, such a thing is logically possible for the class of problems traditionally held within the province of screwing around. What "useful information" was Zappa looking for (in, of all places, *Look*)? He didn't really know and couldn't say. Zappa would have loved the idea of "actionable formats," however. As it turns out, it took him over a year to find a copy of a Varèse record, and when he finally did, he didn't have the money to buy it. He ended up having to convince the salesman to part with it at a discount. Lucky for us, the salesman's "network of transactions" was flawed.

How would Zappa's adventure have played out today? Look Online mentions Varèse, and the "actionable format" is (at best) a click away (and, at worst, over at Pirate Bay). And it's better than that. Amazon says that if you like Varèse, you might also like Messiaen's *Quartet for the End of Time,* which Messiaen actually wrote in a prison camp during the Second World War, the fifth movement of which (the piece, not the war) is based on an earlier piece that uses six Ondes Martenot, which is not only one of the first electronic instruments but possibly the most beautiful sound you have ever heard. And I don't believe this! There's a guy in Seattle who is trying to build an Ondes, and he's already rigged a ring controller to a Q125 Signal Processor. And he's got video.

This is browsing. And it's one of the most venerable techniques in the life of the mind. Ian F. McNeely and Lisa Wolverton make the point forcefully in their book, *Reinventing Knowledge*:

> The categorization of knowledge, whether in tables, trees, or Dewey decimals, has exerted a fascination among modern-day scholars far disproportionate to its actual importance. Classification schemes are arbitrary conveniences. What matters is not whether history is grouped with poetry or with politics and what that says about the ancient mind, but simply whether such schemes make books readily and rapidly accessible to roaming encyclopedic intellects.[15]

It is sometimes forgotten that a search engine doesn't need information to be organized in a way that is at all meaningful to human beings. In fact, a fully automated library—one that uses, say, search engines and robots to retrieve books—would surely not organize things according to subject. Search engines are designed so that the time it takes to locate a text string is as close to constant as possible. Linear ordering is more often a liability in such frameworks, and if we are using robots, it might make more sense to order the physical books by color or size than by subject area.

Libraries today try to facilitate both forms of engagement. The physical card catalog (another technology designed to facilitate serendipitous browsing) has been almost universally replaced with the search engine, and yet the stacks themselves continue to privilege the roaming intellect. It's a sensible compromise, even if we (and more importantly, our students) are more likely to forgo browsing the stacks in favor of searching. Google Books, ironically, tries to do the same thing. Its search engine undoubtedly conceives of the book as a bounded collection of strings within an enormous hash table. Yet on the sidebar, there is a list of subjects and a link labeled "Browse Books." Clicking the latter will take you to an apparently random selection of books within "Classics," "Magazines," "Gardening," "Performing Arts," and others. It will even show you, in a manner vaguely reminiscent of Vannevar Bush's ideas about paths in "As We May Think," "Trending Topics" (books located by other users' search queries).[16]

As a search tool, Google is hard to beat. By providing lookup access to the *content* of the books, it provides a facility that no library has ever been able to offer in the history of the world. Yet as a browsing tool—as a tool for serendipitous engagement—it falls far behind even the most rudimentary library. It can successfully present books on gardening, but because all categorization within Google Books is ultimately a function of search, it has a hard time getting you from gardening to creation myths, from creation myths to Wagner, and from Wagner to Zappa. It may sound perverse to say it, but Google Books (and indeed, most things like it) is simply terrible at browsing. The thing it manages to get right (search) is, regrettably, the one thing that is least likely to turn up something not already prescribed by your existing network of associations. In the end, you're left with a landscape in which the wheel ruts of your roaming intellect are increasingly deepened by habit, training, and preconception. Seek and you shall find. Unfortunately, you probably won't find much else.

What is needed, then, is a full-text archive on the scale of Google Books that is like the vast hypertextual network that surrounds it (and from which it is curiously disconnected). Hand tagging at this scale is neither possible nor desirable; ironically, only algorithmic methods can free us from the tunnel vision that search potentially induces. Without this, the full-text archive becomes something far less than the traditional library.

There are concerns, of course. A humanist scholar—of whatever discipline, and however postmodern—is by definition a believer in shared culture. If everyone is screwing around, one might legitimately wonder whether we can achieve a shared experience of culture sufficient to the tasks we've traditionally set for education—especially matters such as participation in the public square. A media landscape completely devoid of guides and standards is surely as lethal to the life of the mind as one so ramified as to drown out any voice not like one's own. But these concerns are no sooner raised than reimagined by the recent history of the World Wide Web. Today, the dominant format of the web is not the web page but the protean, modded forum: Slashdot, Reddit, Digg, Boing Boing, and countless others. They are guides of a sort, but they describe themselves vaguely as containing "stuff that matters" or "a directory of wonderful things." These sites are at once the product of screwing around and the social network that invariably results when people screw with each other.

As usual, they order this matter better in France. Years ago, Roland Barthes made the provocative distinction between the "readerly text," where one is mostly a passive consumer, and the "writerly text," where, as he put it, the reader, "before the infinite play of the world (the world as function) is traversed, intersected, stopped, plasticized by some singular system (Ideology, Genus, Criticism) which reduces the plurality of entrances, the opening of networks, the infinity of languages."[17] Many have commented on the ways such thoughts appear to anticipate the hypertext, the mashup, and the web. But Barthes himself doubted whether "the pleasure of the text"—the writerly text—could ever penetrate the institutions in which readerly paths through culture are enshrined. He wrote:

> What relation can there be between the pleasure of the text and the institutions of the text? Very slight. The theory of the text postu- lates bliss, but it has little institutional future: what it establishes, its precise accomplishment, its assumption, is a practice (that of the writer), not a science, a method, a research, a pedagogy; on these very principles, this theory can produce only theoreticians or practitioners, not specialists (critics, researchers, professors, students). It is not only the inevitably metalinguistic nature of all institutional research which hampers the writing of textual plea- sure, it is also that we are today incapable of conceiving a true sci- ence of becoming (which alone might assemble our pleasure without garnishing it with a moral tutelage).[18]

Somewhere in there lies a manifesto for how digital humanities might reform certain academic orthodoxies that work against the herme- neutics of screwing around. Have we not already begun to call our- selves "a community of practice," in preference to "a science, a method, a research, a pedagogy"?

But the real message of our technology is, as usual, something en- tirely unexpected—a writerly, anarchic text that is more useful than the readerly, institutional text. Useful and practical not in spite of its anarchic nature but as a natural consequence of the speed and scale that inhere in all anarchic systems. This is, if you like, the basis of the Screwmeneutical Imperative. There are so many books. There is so little time. Your ethical obligation is neither to read them all nor to pretend that you have read them all, but to understand each path through the vast archive as an important moment in the world's duration—as an invitation to community, relationship, and play.

Code, Games, Puppets, and Kleist

I've been unable to get away from these four terms—better, perhaps, to call them mental blocks—for some time. I've been teaching some form of theater history since graduate school. I've been teaching computer programming to students in the arts and humanities for nearly as long. I've been playing games, in one form or another, my whole life. I'm sure my fascination with puppets precedes my ability to walk. At some point along the way, I became aware that you can't think about puppets without thinking about Kleist.

Heinrich von Kleist's 1810 essay "On the Marionette Theater" ("Über das Marionettentheater") is important to students of German Romanticism as well as to students of theater more generally. In it, Kleist approaches a friend—the principal dancer of a local theater—to inquire about his fondness for what Kleist regards as the low and vulgar marionette theaters that were popular in the German marketplaces of the time. His friend replies that a dancer could learn a lot from a puppet.

This is followed by an astoundingly technical discussion of puppetry in which the interlocutor speaks about the key to puppetry lying not in the individual manipulation of the marionette's limbs but in the control of the marionette's center of gravity. Before long, he is speaking of second-order laws of curvature and describing the relationship between the puppeteer's fingers and the marionette as approximating the relationship between numbers and their logarithms or between asymptote and hyperbola. He then goes on to make the astonishing claim that this last bit of human volition could be entirely removed and the dance transferred entirely to the realm of mechanical forces.

It gets stranger and more prescient. Kleist's interlocutor—anticipating discussions of transhumanism by a couple of centuries—confidently avers that the incredible artificial limbs currently being produced by English craftsmen already show the way. "And what," Kleist asks, "is the advantage such a puppet would have over a living dancer?"

> The advantage? First a negative gain, my excellent friend, specifically this: that such a figure would never be affected. For affectation appears, as you know, when the soul (*vis motrix*) locates itself at any point other than the center of gravity of the movement. Because the puppeteer absolutely controls the wire or string, he controls and has power over no other point than this one: therefore all the other limbs are what they should be—dead, pure pendulums following the simple law of gravity, an outstanding quality that we look for in vain in most dancers.
>
> Take for example the dancer P., he continued. When she dances Daphne and is pursued by Apollo, she looks back at him—her soul is located in the vertebrae of the small of her back; she bends as if she were about to break in half, like a naiad from the school of Bernini. And look at the young dancer F. When he dances Paris and stands among the three goddesses and hands the apple to Venus, his soul is located precisely in his elbow, and it is a frightful thing to behold.[1]

There are a few things to notice about this essay. First, and most obviously, it is a philosophical dialogue, and as such, it is of a piece with works like Oscar Wilde's "The Decay of Lying," Marquis de Sade's *Philosophy in the Bedroom,* and, of course, the Platonic dialogues. As in these cases, there is a fictional back-and-forth that probably represents some kind of composite loosely based on actual conversations. But unlike most other examples, the author of this piece appears to come to the interlocutor to be educated, and not the other way around (Socrates has not the slightest expectation of learning what piety is from Euthyphro). In that sense, "On the Marionette Theater" is a bit like *My Dinner with Andre.*

Ultimately, Kleist's dialogue is a discussion about human perfectibility, with the interlocutor suggesting that though Paradise is locked and our backs are to the cherubim, our goal should be to travel the world in the hope that there's a way in through the back. The concerns of Romanticism—a movement that both takes its cue from and rejects earlier enthusiasms concerning rationalism—are here most acute. The essay ends like this:

Now, my excellent friend, said Herr C., you are in possession of everything that is necessary to comprehend what I am saying. We can see the degree to which contemplation becomes darker and weaker in the organic world, so that the grace that is there emerges all the more shining and triumphant. Just as the intersection of two lines from the same side of a point after passing through the infinite suddenly finds itself again on the other side—or as the image from a concave mirror, after having gone off into the infinite, suddenly appears before us again—so grace returns after knowledge has gone through the world of the infinite, in that it appears to best advantage in that human bodily structure that has no consciousness at all—or has infinite consciousness—that is, in the mechanical puppet, or in the God.

Therefore, I replied, somewhat at loose ends, we would have to eat again of the tree of knowledge to fall back again into a state of innocence?

Most certainly, he replied: That is the last chapter of the history of the world.[2]

Games—let us say, for the purposes of this discussion, first-person narrative games of whatever sort—have been likened to many things over the last few decades. Games are like film. Games are like theater. Games are like novels. Games are like films, plays, and novels plus some other things: interactivity, or immersion, or puzzle mechanics. And all of this is perfectly true, to a greater or lesser extent, provided we are looking at them from the front. From the standpoint of the game designer, though, games look very different. From the standpoint of the developer, they are most of all like puppetry.

When I was a kid growing up in Massachusetts, they used to hold what were called "spook walks" around Halloween (I imagine they still do). The idea was that you'd mark out a path through the woods and have a series of local kids (older than you, and therefore automatically terrifying) dress up as zombies or vampires or monsters. They'd jump out at you, spray things at you, make sudden noises, and generally attempt to get you more frightened than you'd already feel walking in the woods in New England at night (alas, there were a lot more dark, wooded areas back then). This isn't, in the end, that much different in kind from *Tony n' Tina's Wedding*—the wildly successful

1988 theater piece by the Artificial Intelligence comedy troupe, in which the audience members are the guests at an Italian American wedding reception.[3]

Both types of theatrical performance are "automatic" to the same degree that any theatrical performance is automatic—even the humblest spook walk has some kind of generalized script controlling what happens, even if you are allowed to go off the trail, pull off your friend's mask, or run away. What's more, any actor can go off script, play the part wrong, or locate their soul in their elbow.

But what if you could, as Kleist's interlocutor suggests, automate the process completely? Imagine! Well, I suppose you'd have the Pirates of the Caribbean ride at Disneyland. Which is to say, you'd have puppets. Crude ones, but puppets that aren't being directly controlled by human beings. I haven't been to a Disney theme park since I was a child, and I assume that today's rides are asymptotically approaching Kleist's asymptotes in terms of center of gravity (and are therefore astonishingly lifelike). That is in part because the code that now replaces the puppeteer's strings is more sophisticated than anything Kleist's interlocutor could possibly have imagined.

Writing a game—and I've tried to write a couple, though no blockbusters, alas—is rather exactly like writing an automated spook walk with programming code. The player experiences the game as a series of rooms, or tunnels, or chambers populated with objects and characters. The programmer conceives of the game as a series of discrete states, the transitions between which are triggered by some input from the user (or the passage of time). You seem to have passed through a door unimpeded. In fact, you have walked through an invisible collider that has not only caused a piece of ceiling tile to fall on the other side of the room but that has notified several other parts of the code that this event has occurred. You seem to have picked up an object. What you've actually done is sent an anonymous function to a puzzle you haven't encountered yet that allows you to solve it (assuming that that puzzle has received all the other signals that enable it). This is painstaking work—every bit as hard as filming a scene in a movie, except that while there are lights, and cameras, and props, and perhaps actors, the entire thing is controlled using one single control mechanism. In the end, even you—the programmer—won't "operate" it in any real sense at all.

It should come as no surprise, then, that the rhetoric of game programming eerily resembles the theme of Kleist's interlocutor (and here, I'm talking not about academic game studies but about the sort of discussion that takes place on game developer sites like Gamasutra or at game developer conferences). In the most obvious sense, it is a discourse that echoes Alfred North Whitehead's statement that "civilization advances by extending the number of important operations which we can perform without thinking of them"—a statement so shot through with Enlightenment assumptions about the capabilities of human reasoning that it could have been written by Hume.[4] Someone had to figure out how to get realistic-looking water out of a graphics card. Modern game programmers don't think about this at all, because the game engine does it for them. The AI algorithms that make it so the same number of fighter jets do not attack you at the same time in the same way over and over have been known for decades, though they once represented a serious research problem. The assumption, therefore, is that we are approaching not merely the moment of perfect verisimilitude but the moment in which Grace appears most perfectly in its utter lack of human consciousness. We are striving, in other words, toward perfect puppetry.

I doubt very much that any modern game designer would put it that way. I doubt even more that any would say that we are therefore finding the back door to the Garden of Eden. But they might agree that the power of games—the reason we need to treat them not as low and vulgar art but as something worthy of our deepest attention as students of human culture—lies in the fact that it relies precisely on the moment in which what we regard as the hard center of human consciousness meets its purest form of absence. To put that less ornately: we (game designers) are getting better and better at making things that have no consciousness manipulate your consciousness as a player, because the entire process is getting easier (more mechanized). And the result of this collision between the human and the mechanical is not the comic, as Bergson suggests, but the dramatic. The fact that you probably can't name any famous game designers, or (even if you're a gamer) only a few, is not because games haven't achieved the same cultural status as theater and film. It is because the game designer is trying to disappear in the same way that Kleist's interlocutor suggests puppeteers might disappear.[5]

My students, at this point, are always eager to point out that there's still an author here—there's still a human mind behind that gorgeously rendered waterfall, even if the machine can compute everything about it, including things that are greater than the sum of their parts (modern physics engines allow you to say, "Put some water here"—the babbling brook with perfect patterns of ripples and eddies need not concern the programmer any longer). And my students are surely right. Someone has to design the Pirates, even if the ride itself runs on rails. There is a story in most games, and people come up with those stories much in the same way that people have been coming up with stories since people first started telling stories (even if there are whiteboards and managers involved).

The difference, though, is that the author is trying to disappear much in the way that nineteenth-century European novelists were trying to disappear (by eschewing the narrative interruptions of a Cervantes or a Henry Fielding). Even now, we still take as axiomatic the position taken by Infocom (maker of the text adventure games that still influence game design today, and to which I was completely addicted in the eighties). As they wrote in their marketing materials in 1984, "As hard as we work on perfecting our stories, we always leave out one essential element—the main character. And that's where you come in. Once you've loaded Infocom's interactive fiction into your computer, you experience something akin to waking up inside a story."[6] As graphics get better, as algorithms get smarter, as game engines get easier to use, it becomes easier to put someone in that bed.

Is this wide-eyed, triumphalist march of progress any different from the history of technical theater? At the beginning of *A Doll's House,* Ibsen writes an extraordinarily detailed set of stage directions in which every prop from the carpet to the porcelain figures in the étagère are described in meticulous detail. All of this was, of course, well within the ambit of nineteenth-century stage design. But he also includes another set direction: *"A winter's day."*[7] How did Ibsen pull that one off? Well, there's a scene where the characters—in what we might assume to be classic Stanislavskian manner—come in through the door shivering and make much of the fact that it's cold outside. Today, though, you'd also talk to a lighting designer, who would not only cast winter light through the windows but ask you what time it is, whether there's snow on the ground, and whether it's overcast. Ibsen would have given anything for this ability.

But the history of lighting technology is not at all like the history of software development. All software is built on a series of abstractions from the primitive to the more elaborate. Each time we add an abstraction, we make the abstraction beneath it disappear—"extending the number of important operations which we can perform without thinking of them," as Whitehead puts it. Theater lighting progressed from natural lighting, to dipped candles, to chandeliers, to gas lights, to electrical lights, to electrical lights with smoke machines, lasers, and gels. Electrical lights represent an innovation with respect to gas lights, but incandescent bulbs are not an abstraction built on top of gas lights.

What happens, then, when the *story,* the thing we most regard as *not* part of the ever-rising chain of abstractions, becomes another thing we can perform without thinking? The first thing to say about that, of course, is that it has already happened. The story of a game like *Portal* or *Grand Theft Auto* is mostly an emergent property that arises from the mostly automated puppetry behind the scenes—a phenomenon even more evident in game mods where the basic pieces of the game and its mechanics are reassembled (with virtually no programming at all) into a new story. But where, one might ask, are the *real* stories? Where is the *Middlemarch* of games?

If you think that proposition absurd, I would ask you to recall the state of the European novel at the beginning of the eighteenth century—a cheap, vulgar genre mainly good for porn. It is telling, too, that as this move toward ever higher forms of abstraction advances, our collective anxiousness more and more resembles earlier worries about the rise of fiction in the West. Stories about teenagers who don't eat, sleep, or take showers because they're too deep into *Assassin's Creed*—or worse, armed students following the irresistible dictates of *Call of Duty* into a middle school—mirror those worries about the effect that romances were having on people (young women especially) going back to the early modern period. Somehow, in the course of a few centuries, we went from thinking that novels were dangerous, to posters in which Kermit the Frog (a puppet) exhorts children to read. But this fear runs deep in Western culture. Fiction is lying. Fiction induces trance. Fiction makes the body vulnerable. Fiction fills your head with silly ideas utterly divorced from reality.

I have been suggesting—and I am hardly the first—that Kleist was at least two centuries ahead of his time. But perhaps the converse is also true: that we are, spiritually speaking, at least two centuries before ours when it comes to thinking about games. For all our talk of a new age (a "digital age" populated by "digital natives"), games are, in the end, the dream of the Enlightenment and indicate how profoundly we remain drenched in its ideals. We write games about mindless AIs taking over the world (entities that, naturally, must be defeated by the power of humanness), using fully unconscious bits of pure logic and mathematics that, because they are built into chains of abstraction, begin to exhibit properties of emergence. If it is hard to discern where Kleist really stands—convinced by his interlocutor or satirizing the entire line of thought—it is because he himself was undoubtedly torn, as we are, between reason and what the ancients called "the passions." Or to put that only slightly differently, we are torn between Enlightenment and Romanticism. We are drawn to perfect marionettes even as we are repelled by them.

One often hears charges of "technological utopianism" (or something similarly derogatory) directed toward digital humanists, game designers, and technologists in general, and to the degree that computer technology represents the dream of the Enlightenment, the charge is an appropriate one. Such utopianism does not, however, represent the sudden appearance of a dangerous ideology among a large group of benighted enthusiasts. Rather, it correctly identifies a subspecies of an inescapable influence on our collective center of gravity that has been dominating Western consciousness for centuries. We still desire perfect rationality—perfect replacement of our broken tendency toward "affectation."

But that desire competes (again, always and inescapably) with our desire to resist this replacement. Contemporary cultural studies, mostly looking at games from the front, undertakes this resistance by attempting to explain the way in which games enact wider cultural phenomena or the precise manner in which a game manipulates the player's thoughts and emotions in a manner best understood within the realm of the political. But this is merely a highly refracted form of the dream of the Romantics—emancipation through awareness. It is interested in showing you the way you (or, less precisely, "other people") are being carefully manipulated and duped.

The move is hardly confined to game studies. Strindberg is trying to convince you that you are in Sweden. The literary critic proceeds from the notion that you are not, by showing you the wires of Strindberg's art. Break out of the trance (we say to our students); the moment in which Jean kisses Miss Julie's boot is wrapped up in dizzyingly complex interactions between gender and power that are not at all as they might appear. Does such investigation require an understanding of the interaction between medium, genre, and culture? Of course it does. But what if the medium of a game—the back of a game—is qualitatively unlike the "back" of other artistic forms?

To return to an earlier point: oil paint does not build on the abstraction of tempera. The steady cam isn't an object that can forget about the cam. Free indirect discourse is not an affordance Jane Austen and Gustave Flaubert gained because the "problem" of ordinary indirect speech had been solved. What's more, artists regularly go back to tempera, filmmakers to eight-millimeter handhelds, and novelists to third-person accounts dotted with the moralizing interruptions that permeate *Don Quixote* and *Tom Jones*. This is seldom the case with code. Absent some other motive, game designers going for that retro, 8-bit look do not pull out an assembler from the days of Atari and start again; they fire up a modern game engine that can do in seconds what took the Atari engineers years to accomplish. Here, we're merely talking about the nature of the computational medium. If we accept that there is a connection, however shifting and ambiguous, between medium, genre, and culture, then the media of gaming—the ways in which it, unlike previous artistic media, is built on what amounts to an architecture of subsumption—must change the way we think about the tension between front and back. Is the game designer tricking you? Of course. So was Shakespeare. But the tools with which those tricks are played are following a historical logic without precise analogue elsewhere.

Perhaps I am open to the charge of trying to impose a narrow form of structuralism on game studies—a kind of materialist poetics for the age of *Bioshock*. But most critical approaches to code have merely moved the back to the front—thus revealing that the basic findings of cultural studies are as true of code as they are of *The Sopranos*. That would be a natural and even comforting discovery if television as a medium worked like code as a medium. My contention is that it does not.

Does that mean that we should stop looking at games from the front? Surely not. Neither is it the case that games can't be understood without knowledge of the back—a line of thinking every bit as facile as the suggestion that one can't properly drive a car without knowledge of the how the clutch works. My suggestion is perhaps nothing more than what Kleist's interlocutor almost says: a humanist could learn a lot from a game engine.

The Art of DH

Sometime around the turn of the millennium, I gave a talk in Germany about mapping the scenes in Shakespeare's plays. I won't say that I was the first person ever to produce network graphs of literary works with a computer, but I was pretty early to the game.

Essentially, I wrote a program that could take encoded versions of Shakespeare plays and turn them into colorful maps.[1] Formally, they were what in mathematics are called cyclic directed graphs and, when treated as such, had sets of properties like width, planarity, number of cycles, number of degrees, and chromatic numbers. With the help of a graduate student at the Graduate School of Library and Information Science at the University of Illinois named Bei Yu, I wrote a program that could analyze the graphs, figure out all of those properties, and write the numbers into a table. We then assigned the plays some labels: tragedy, comedy, history, and romance. The question, then, was this: Could we take these properties, relate them to genre, and use them to predict the genre of an unknown instance? Or, to put that another way, could I get the computer to figure out the genre of a play based solely on low-level structural properties (like the number of scenes, the number of connections, the number of consecutive scenes, and so forth)?

The answer was "yes" and "no." And the "no" was way, way more interesting.

By and large, the machine learning algorithm could do it. In fact, it was able to classify every play in Shakespeare's corpus save two: *Othello* and *Romeo and Juliet.* The computer insisted that these two plays were comedies. And that's interesting, because Shakespeare scholars have the same trouble. In 1979, Susan Snyder authored a book entitled *The Comic Matrix of Shakespeare's Tragedies,* which I can easily summarize: "Has anyone noticed that *Othello* and *Romeo and Juliet* have the structure of comedy?"[2] The computer wasn't getting it wrong; the computer was getting it uncannily right.

Now, there's much to discuss here. But I tell this story only partially as a way of framing the questions this kind of project raises for the humanities. When I think about this project, the main thing I think about is not whether I got the scene divisions right, or whether our data mining algorithms were sound, but a question that someone asked during the Q&A after the talk. This was before I had done the genre detector; at that stage in the history of DH—back when it was still being called "humanities computing"—you could actually get up and amaze an audience of text-analysis scholars with a network graph.

Anyway, one of those scholars asked me a question I wasn't expecting at all and haven't been asked since: "Is this just art?"

He didn't mean it as a compliment; in fact, he sounded mildly pissed off. What he meant, of course, is that these were nothing more than pretty pictures. Perhaps he might have been mollified by the later work on genre, but the question still stood. I don't recall what sort of thing I stammered in response, but I know for sure what I was thinking: What if it is? What would be so bad about that?

Everything I've done since—every bit of theoretical musing on digital humanities—has had this irritating question in the background. How we answer it, it seems to me, helps to decide where we stand in relation to various epistemologies (including positivism and scientism), what we think scholarship is for, and how we imagine computation playing a role in humanistic inquiry. The question also led me, eventually (and to my surprise), to making art.

As I said, I haven't been asked this question since, but I've seen countless instances in which digital humanities touches a nerve. Figuring out exactly which nerve has been my life's work. But the negative reactions are legion. I could do no better at this point than to quote Matthew Kirschenbaum's glorious précis of the detractions:

Digital humanities digs MOOCs. Digital humanities is an artifact of the post-9/11 security and surveillance state (the NSA of the MLA). Like Johnny, digital humanities can't read. Digital humanities doesn't do theory. Digital humanities *never* historicizes. Digital humanities is complicit. Digital humanities is naive. Digital humanities is hollow huckster boosterism. Digital humanities is managerial. Digital humanities is the academic import of Silicon Valley solutionism (the term that is the shibboleth of bad-boy tech critic Evgeny Morozov). Digital humanities cannot abide critique. Digital humanities appeals to those in search of an oasis from the concerns of race, class, gender, and sexuality. Digital humanities does not inhale (easily the best line of the bunch). Digital humanities wears Google Glass. Digital humanities wears thick, thick glasses (guilty). Perhaps most damning of all: digital humanities is something separate from the rest of the humanities, and—this is the real secret— digital humanities *wants* it that way.[3]

I'm sure I could track down the tweet, blog post, essay, or random screed in which each of these charges is leveled, and I can say that Kirschenbaum—ever the mild-mannered and gracious scholar—isn't fully capturing the biliousness with which these coals are heaped on our heads.

What do I think? I think it's nonsense, of course. *Never* historicizes? The entire field is in open flight from race, gender, class, and sexuality? Kirschenbaum goes on to make the argument that all of these critiques are directed at a vague *construct*—none of them are willing to address particular *things*: projects, archives, websites, work. Because if they did, they'd have to acknowledge engagement with these subjects, plenty of theorizing and self-reflection, and a good bit of internal anxiety about the very things of which we are being accused. A perfectly self-critical community free of headiness and thoughtlessness? Hardly. But I am not aware of many scholarly communities that have a book series that is essentially devoted to self-critique.[4]

I think a still deeper thing underlies these critiques, though, and it speaks to the issues I mentioned a moment ago. What is the humanities about? What is the nature of its particular type of inquiry? And most importantly, where does it stand in relationship to the Scylla of Science, on the one hand, and the Charybdis of Art, on the other?

It is often forgotten that the humanities emerged out of art in general and belletristic writing in particular. Through most of history, we witness the overriding sense that people thought of things like literary criticism and history as sharing some kind of essential nature with things like novels, plays, personal essays, and even poetry. Certainly, in the ancient world—and well into the early modern period— the idea that there was a thing called "history" that was categorically different from, say, philosophy was mostly unknown. This isn't to say that there was no sense of genre, but only that all of these things were thought to be somehow joined, and not merely because they were written down. Even into the twentieth century, when Ezra Pound and T. S. Eliot were calling for a renewed literary criticism, I believe they were thinking in these much broader terms.

The idea of an English department that also, by the way, does creative writing—but the lit people don't, you know, hang out with the creative writers or even know what they're really up to—is a quite recent invention, and it represents a conscious attempt to create a discipline (and hence a generic practice) that is fully distinct from art. If you doubt that, write a personal essay on what *Long Day's Journey into Night* means to you, and try to publish it in a scholarly journal.

And the phenomenon is hardly confined to my own area of study. In a modern history department, "narrative history"—the kind most people actually read—is almost a curse word, even though it is the oldest kind of historical writing. Anglo-American philosophy departments are at this point so steeped in analytical philosophy that much so-called continental philosophy is scarcely regarded as germane to the subject. Art history—the discipline that can count Giorgio Vasari among its alumni—is similarly in open flight from anything that seems too close to the object of study.

Is this a bad thing? I'd like to place that question in abeyance and simply acknowledge it as a soft, ever-present disciplinary fear. But it's one that pales in comparison to the other fear: the previously mentioned Scylla of Science. And while science had more trouble inserting itself into the curriculum than is often acknowledged, it now seems clear that science "won" in some fundamental sense. Apparently immune from questions about "what you're going to do with that," funded in terms that humanists can scarcely fathom, and blessed with all the public-relations glory of "discoveries," contemporary science rules the roost of the contemporary research university. What's more, it is a dark but undeniable secret that the very cheap humanities funds the very expensive sciences at the curricular level at most institutions. It's been called "physics envy," and we all have it.

Except that at another level, we don't have it at all. If we are at pains to distinguish ourselves from the arts, we are similarly at pains to proclaim our methodological independence from the sciences. We don't *do* science. We don't want to do science. We just want a bit of their glamour.

What nerve does DH touch? This latter one: this fear of an arid scientism being brought to bear on the objects of humanistic inquiry. And despite Kirschenbaum's trenchant reflections on the matter, a thoughtful critic can find a raging positivist in the DH community as easily as someone working on race. In fact, the positivist gets all the press, because sending ten thousand novels through a machine makes for a better story both for news outlets who, for once, are reporting on what a humanist is doing and for magazines like the *New Republic* and the *Los Angeles Review of Books* that delight in identifying DH as the source of most of what is going wrong in contemporary humanities departments.

What I'd like to suggest—and it's a bold suggestion, I think—is that rather than becoming a scientized version of itself through the digital humanities, the humanities should rediscover and reembrace its deep connection with the arts. In fact, I'd like to see this become the central methodological imperative of the digital humanities. I'd even like to suggest that doing so might help us with some of the thorny practical matters of how to evaluate work in DH.

Back to Shakespeare for a moment. I believe that any resemblance my work on that project had with scientific inquiry was mostly superficial. The main commonality with science was a concern with measurement—the foundational methodological component of all the sciences. Computers are good at measuring things. More crucially, they demand that we measure. The computer simply will not tolerate any equivocation about scene divisions or genres. It understands nothing at all about the contingency of truth claims. It is as if, after we've made all the right noises about indeterminacy and the unrecoverability of performance practices, the computer says, "Great. What are the damn scenes?"

But I believe that rather than "scientizing" the humanities, this always-necessary measurement procedure is one of the things that can most invigorate our engagement with humanistic materials. There's a crucial difference between waving your hands over something (however engaging that gesture might be in practice) and having to *decide* one way or the other. The computer makes you decide. Studying gender? Eventually, we'll be *counting* the pronouns. Interested in place?

The computer wants an actual map. Think you know which authors have richer vocabularies, choppier sentences, or more consonant lines? Again and again, we find out that we don't. What I'm describing here is the consequence of a severe *limitation* of the computer—a constraint, but one that is almost always entirely productive in nature. Computers are fast, obedient, and stupid. People are slow, rebellious, and smart. Together, we can probe the fate of the handsome, clever, and rich in ways that were completely unimaginable a few decades ago, precisely because the computer forces us to see and work in ways that we're not used to seeing and working.

To do that, though, we need to release ourselves from the idea that the "result" is what matters (or that this business of "deciding" things leads inexorably to some previously unattainable stability). My data mining experiments with Shakespeare's genres seemed exciting at the time, but didn't I merely affirm what was already widely believed? The real excitement, the real usefulness, the truly humanistic part of the exercise, was *creating* the graphs and poring over them. That exercise made me think about Shakespeare's scenes in ways that I never had and produced exactly what we want in a humanistic discussion: questions. Lots of them.

We all recognize the outlines of this essential procedure because we do it all the time as teachers. We say, "Turn to page 95. Now let's look at the passage on 68." We tell our students to pay attention to just the female characters, or just the narrator, or to think about and discuss some underlying motif. In each case, I would argue that we are providing productive constraints in which to think. The computer can't replace all or even most elements of that process, and I, for one, don't want it to. But its own jarring, relentless constraints are hard to find elsewhere. When I first shifted from making charts and graphs to theorizing about them, I took to calling them "preinterpretative objects." You can imagine how well that went over. But what I was trying to get at is this idea of a cut-up, deformed, partial, deliberately constrained view of something that, ironically, allows us to see.

Did I just define art? Probably not, but one can hope. And this brings me to my very unlikely second theme, which is how I went from analyzing art to making it.

My colleague Brian Pytlik-Zillig and I became collaborators five minutes after we first met (over fifteen years ago). There was no thought of collaborating on art; we were both interested in text analysis and visualization. But we had secret lives: Brian as a visual artist, and I as a composer. Making art was never just a hobby or a sideline for either of us, but we kept it from our colleagues, and mostly from each other. That is, until Brian started playing around with SVG.

Brian, ever the midwesterner, is naturally humble and self-deprecating, so let me say what he would never say: he's almost certainly the best XSLT programmer in the world, and he's doing things with SVG that push so hard against the envelope of what it was designed to do, that he (a) had to develop his own gargantuan tool to do it and (b) can barely find rendering engines capable of carrying off his ideas. Initially, he was making little animations to test and stretch the capabilities of his system so he could use that system to do text-analysis visualization. But you shouldn't imagine that these test animations looked like pie charts and scatter plots. They were rather closer to Brian's own practice as a visual artist: strange, bracing, often surrealistic images that variously drew on issues involving disability, childhood, and the not-always-obvious beauty of the American Midwest.

I knew what he was doing, and I remember walking into his office one day and saying, "These are really great, but they're, you know, awfully quiet. What if I wrote a score for one of them?" The rest isn't history, so much as an alternate timeline that made us fear slightly for our careers, as these pieces rapidly became a major preoccupation for both of us.[5]

But what is it that was so different? I started out as an orchestral composer, and though it might not seem like it (given the dizzying range of material in common practice Western music), there are rules and constraints. Lots and lots of them. Beard-stroking microtonal experiments aside (and there are rules there too), there aren't twelve semitones in an octave one day and fourteen the next. Some intervals are dissonant, some aren't, and the logic of how that works was worked out centuries ago. One of my favorite books on composing is a book called *Gradus ad Parnassum* by the eighteenth-century composer Johann Joseph Fux (1660–1741). It is written as a dialogue between a teacher (Aloysius) and his student Josephus and begins as follows:

> JOSEPHUS: I come to you, venerable master, in order to be introduced to the rules and principles of music.

ALOYSIUS: You want, then, to learn the art of composition?

JOSEPHUS: Yes.

ALOYSIUS: But are you not aware that this study is like an immense ocean, not to be exhausted even in the lifetime of a Nestor?[6]

Despite that rather forbidding start, Aloysius then proceeds to explain in the most orderly and concise way possible the principles of counterpoint (which is the technical matter of writing two or more independent melodic lines against one another). The book comes close to exhausting the subject in 140 pages. The fact that I could still profit from a book like this, written in 1725, when I was starting out, tells the whole story. The truth is that while orchestral music has changed in ways that would have been unimaginable to Fux, the rules of counterpoint haven't changed much at all, and every composer—no matter how "experimental"—still uses them to some degree.

The process of composition, therefore, is not unlike the process of using a computer to see things in a new way. "Write a piece that goes with these images" is like saying, "Make a scary game," or "Write a happy story." We have to get more specific, find a system we can think and work in, get some rules. To choose one example: In one of our early pieces, there's an old car driving down a road. So I had something like straight, flat Nebraska highways in mind, and maybe spare instrumentation like a wind trio (which is still in the realm of "Write a happy story"). Somehow, fiddling around with that led me to car horns. Car horns are second intervals (or at least, they sound that way to me). Before long I was in the weeds of appoggiaturas and fugal passages—exactly the kinds of constraints that can produce art.

More recent pieces might not sound like it, but they are musically even more heavily constrained. None of our work is "algorithmic"; at some level, it's all very precisely controlled and deliberate. But we made a commitment early on to using only laptops to create our pieces, and that includes the music. In early work, I was actually writing scores on ordinary manuscript paper, but that has almost entirely dropped away. I do not record sounds or play instruments to create the audio, and in fact, I do not even have a MIDI keyboard in my studio. I tend to use step sequencers and other software-only gadgets to create melodic lines, and happy accidents abound. *Generative* would be a better word for the way we work. Or *emergent*. Though terms like these imply that one is creating a set of initial conditions and letting it run. Our pieces are almost obsessively "wrought" frame by frame.

How like the process of working with computers to study the human record. Once again, we find a space in which to think and then use that space to think some more. All the while, the form—the code, the API—is imposing rules (sometimes for us to break) that ironically lead to creativity. How, too, like the process of teaching our students to read or think critically. None of us begin our classes with "What did you think of the book?" We temporarily narrow our students' vision in order to expand it.

I should probably square the circle that I've been drawing around art, the humanities, and DH a bit more securely, so let me close with a few observations.

Let us first admit that the digital humanities' plan for world domination is a fiction mostly made up by people who aren't actually doing it. The largest gathering of digital humanists I've ever attended (and I've attended lots of them) had considerably fewer than a thousand people present, and that included representatives of literally every branch of the humanities from dozens of countries. That DH punches way above its weight is partially an artifact of its novelty (though it is nowhere near as new as people suppose) and partially the result of its unlikely and, depending on who you talk to, thrilling and terrifying connection to the sciences.

What I've tried to suggest, though, is that the real meaning of DH—or perhaps just my solemn hope for it—has to do with its unlikely connection to the long-lost arts. If we decide that the products of work in DH are not meant to be "results" in the conventional sense—if we come to see them more as provocations born of systems of constraint into which scholars enter and from which arise invitations into those provocations, if we choose to view the activity this way, then perhaps we can come to see that the real virtue of DH bears a stronger resemblance to artistic practice than it does to scientific methodology. And if I'm right about that—or if I could be right about that in the future—then might DH help us find our way back to this forbidden alliance with the arts themselves? Our way of evaluating this work might also benefit from looking to models in the fine and performing arts. I am hardly the only one who thinks the standard write-review-publish model doesn't feel right in DH, and while I admire the many thoughtful attempts to make it conform, I haven't seen anything capacious enough to embrace the full range of activity. The studio art model, in which "number of pieces created" is not necessarily the right metric, might make a lot more sense. Right now, poster sessions are thought of by some (quite wrongly, I think) as the venue for people who, you know, couldn't get a real paper into the conference. The fact that most people walk away from the poster session at DH conferences pretty convinced that some of the work was better than what they heard on the panels should give us a clue. What about a DH group show? What about juried showcases? Or something that looks more like a science fair than a humanities conference? There's perhaps no getting around the need to somehow measure the influence a particular provocation is having, but most of the digital humanists I know find themselves in the strange position of having a wildly popular website, resource, or tool and a merit review committee asking who the publisher is. For those people, "number of hits" isn't necessarily a bad thing.

Perhaps the most important thing here, though, is the role played by DH practitioners who have tenure. If we're going to have a conversation about whether a database is a scholarly object, and whether scholarship need always be so divorced from the concerns of art, we need professors submitting databases, visualizations, websites, tools, and even things that follow the logic of art to review committees. What can I say? As an English professor who teaches programming and software engineering while writing music and making films, I can only say that after a while they decide that your weirdness isn't going away and that they will have to learn to operate under this highly productive constraint.

Digital Humanities and
Its Disconnects

Digital humanities has come under intense criticism over the years from a variety of different quarters and for a variety of different reasons. Few critiques, however, seem to me as brutal as Alan Liu's:

> It is as if, when the order comes down from the funding agencies, university administrations, and other bodies mediating today's dominant socioeconomic and political beliefs, digital humanists just concentrate on pushing the "execute" button on projects that amass the most data for the greatest number, process that data most efficiently and flexibly (flexible efficiency being the hallmark of postindustrialism), and manage the whole through ever "smarter" standards, protocols, schema, templates, and databases uplifting Frederick Winslow Taylor's original scientific industrialism into ultraflexible postindustrial content management systems camouflaged as digital editions, libraries, and archives—all without pausing to reflect on the relation of the whole digital juggernaut to the new world order.[1]

Godwin's Law notwithstanding, there are surely few curses one could pronounce upon an academic endeavor more devastating than the charge that it is merely a more subtle form of Taylorism. For Liu—and, indeed, for all who directly or indirectly charge digital humanities with being "undertheorized"—the problem is not merely that digital humanists are behaving uncritically (that would be damning enough) but that in doing so they are becoming complicit in the very structures that camouflage postindustrial juggernauts. "To be an equal partner," digital humanists will need to show that "thinking critically about metadata, for instance, scales into thinking critically about the power, finance, and other governance protocols of the world."[2] That is the admonishment that gives rise to the title of the attack, its question, and its urgent exhortation: "Where Is Cultural Criticism in the Digital Humanities?"

Liu's essay is more nuanced than this, and his essential outlook on the future of the digital humanities is more hopeful. Yet anyone involved with digital humanities might suppose that their own superego—that voice that is quieted only by complete absorption in the gory details of implementation—had written that paragraph. Digital humanities has sometimes tried to describe itself innocently as a set of methodologies or as being mostly concerned with infrastructure, but no cultural critic would think such matters innocent (and what humanist is not, if only by temperament, a cultural critic?). *Methodology, infrastructure, algorithm, mechanism*—these are the terms that underlie statist bureaucracy, scientific management, and those unthinking and uncontrolled processes that, in our imaginings of the future, escape their human masters to wreak unforeseen havoc on the products of that same purposefulness. Failing to live the examined life in the face of such possibility fails, in the language of geekery, to fulfill the Prime Directive.

Answering these charges, though, is a lot harder than it sounds. And much depends on how we answer it, since it appears to lie at the heart of that most troublesome of questions: "What is digital humanities?" Here, presented in composite form, are a few of the possibilities that have been offered for how digital humanities (whatever it might be) might attend the banquet clothed in the proper garment:

- Digital humanities should stop resisting its status as a service discipline but should instead politicize that service through direct social action. In this version of DH, tools and frameworks self-consciously dismiss their apparent status as value-neutral objects and become tools used for explicit, activist interventions.
- Digital humanities will realize its proper political nature by engaging in particular areas of study to which it is presently not or only weakly committed: the study of race, gender, class, and the devastating effects of colonialism, but also critical pedagogy, recovery of minority literatures and artifacts, and the various "gaps in the archive" that render the conclusions of such projects as text analysis and data mining of large textual corpora unreliable, if not nakedly false.

- Since digital humanities cannot escape its entrenchment in the structures of power (corporate, globalist, neoliberal, etc.), it must at least assume political responsibility by developing a robust understanding of the ways in which creating and using digital tools implicates those who do such things (including digital humanists themselves) in various structures of power. Cultural theory and cultural studies are the most well-developed instruments for cultivating that self-awareness, and digital humanists would do well to avail themselves of these frameworks.

I hope it is obvious that none of these proposals are straw men. All have been made, in one way or another, by thoughtful critics of digital humanities from without and within the field. Still, the difficulties they raise are not cavils.

A digital humanities recalibrated as a form of explicit activism might serve to resolve a long-standing difficulty within the academy. By the time cultural studies arose, the Marxism from which it drew much of its initial fervor had been transformed into "Marxianism"—less a plan for explicit revolution and more a hermeneutical procedure by which the terms of the totally administered society might be examined. With the idea that culture (as opposed to, or in conjunction with, economics) might be the primary manifestation of such administration, cultural studies turned itself not only toward mass culture but to the view (unimaginable to the Frankfurt School, though still consistent with historical materialism) that consumers of mass culture might be a source of revolutionary pressure. In this way, culture itself might conceivably become the source from which revolution eventually springs. Even so, cultural studies eventually came to understand itself as being largely concerned with critique. When *Marxism and the Interpretation of Culture* appeared—the first of many readers intended to articulate the terms on which cultural studies rests—"the definition of *activism* was radically narrowed and hemmed in, referring only to textualised interpretative activity."[3]

"Breaking down barriers" was a new metaphorical task for this Marxism, not to be confused with attacking the barricades; its purpose was to add political, historical, economic, and theoretical dimensions to interpretative analysis of culture (the latter understood broadly as "discourses . . . art . . . beliefs . . . social practices . . . psychology"). This was a *reading* practice.[4]

It has been so ever since.

The development of software is not, by itself, a reading practice, but neither is it an obvious form of protest. "Hacktivism," concrete attempts at bridging the digital divide, and even black-hat hacking might conceivably return humanistic inquiry to protest, activism, and civil disobedience (of the sort that characterized the work of the earliest members of the Frankfurt School, for example). Far from being merely a group of intellectuals talking to other intellectuals, such actions might literally intervene in the world outside the academy. Nonetheless, few if any existing digital projects within the humanities are so engaged.

That digital humanities as a discipline might poorly represent (or even be openly hostile to), say, race and gender studies would be a lamentable situation to say the least, but identifying that deficiency doesn't at all serve to address the theoretical problem of how creating digital objects relates to cultural criticism as such. If anything, it supports the (in Liu's view, false) assumption that building and making can successfully address the problem. Adeline Koh's site, Digitizing "Chinese Englishmen": Representations of Race and Empire in the Nineteenth Century—an early product of the loosely organized but rhetorically powerful #transformDH movement—is unusually explicit about its attempt to build and make in order to repair:

> Our idea of the archive comes from the "Postcolonial Studies" group, such as Edward Said, Gayatri Spivak, Partha Chatterjee and Sara Suleri, who argued in the 1980s that the West had "Orientalized," or created powerful derogatory stereotypes of non-white people prevalent throughout its literature, art and culture, or "archive." The "Postcolonial Studies" group argued for a rereading of this literature, art and culture, or what V. Y. Mudimbe termed the rereading of the "colonial library,"—a cultural repository of information that had become the "archive" for representing people of non-European descent.[5]

Koh cites a number of cultural critics, but whether the archive is itself an act of cultural criticism is another matter. That the project arose from theoretical engagement is beyond doubt, but it is not at all clear how the creation of an archive (as opposed to a book or an article) is not already compromised by the forces Liu identifies.

Here, as elsewhere, "content" (contra McLuhan) is thought to be enough to absolve one from such objections—that it provides a way in which one can be exempt from "pushing the execute button" in precisely the same way that any other project does. Rereading the art and culture of Europe for the ways in which it "Orientalizes" people of non-European descent is, without doubt, an act of cultural criticism. Building and making an archive—writing the software upon which it is instantiated, for example, or preparing images for display—is not necessarily so. Critics of DH like Liu might be forcing us into the un-comfortable position of considering such things as the decolonization of the archive—an obviously laudable and necessary act—as simply another form of postindustrial efficiency. But even if it were a matter of content, the failure of others to engage in similar acts of redress would merely suggest lack of awareness about the possibilities of digi-tal practice, not a failure to theorize that practice or transform it into cultural critique. The solution to gaps in the archive is to fill those gaps. The solution to the problem of a lack of tools for postcolonial studies is to build those tools. Even if there exists a complete lack of awareness on the part of practitioners concerning how to build those tools, gaining that awareness does not automatically transform the activity into critiquing and interpreting.

Such projects only raise the stakes of Liu's most serious demand: that digital humanities develop a sense of awareness and self-reflection about its own activity using the existing frameworks of critical the-ory and cultural studies. The problem, in Liu's view, lies not with the inability of DH to engage in direct social action or to countenance demands that it represent minority voices and concerns but in its ap-parent inability to critique itself and, in the process, instantiate a form of political meaning. The problem, once again, is that it appears not to contemplate such questions at all.

This is not a substanceless objection. While we can make no sure assumptions about the inner lives of those engaged with metadata protocols, archives, and data mining, such projects very often leave no trace whatsoever of any theoretical musings that might have oc-curred. Discursive metaobjects in which connections are made be-tween the higher and lower criticism (now recast in terms of big theory and little building) are rare; when they appear, it is usually to remind the viewer or user of the interpretative, contingent nature of the work in question. Such apologias are undoubtedly necessary, but it is difficult to avoid the suspicion that the moment of reflection in these cases has more to do with hedging charges against facile beliefs in objective representation, or even an attempt to proleptically avert the digital equivalent of those nineteenth- and early twentieth-century exhibits in natural history museums that we now find embarrassing and offensive. It is difficult to imagine any kind of footnote in which the project's complicity in, say, globalism is confidently asserted, let alone dilated at length.

Even the volume in which Liu's essay appears, *Debates in the Digital Humanities,* contains not one chapter in which the creation of digital tools—the act of building and making them—is explicitly characterized as cultural critique. Digital humanities is defined, its inclusiveness as a discipline questioned, its pedagogical protocols imagined, its future predicted, but nothing in the entire volume (including Liu's own chapter) actually transforms building within the digital humanities into reflection on globalism, corporatism, neoliberalism, capitalism, or any other macroexpansion of ideology. Even a section entitled "Critiquing the Digital Humanities" addresses only the first two of the composite suggestions I have offered above. No one suggests (at least in that volume) that digital humanities do with their tools and websites what the Frankfurt School or the Birmingham School did for the academic episteme. One may critique DH, but nowhere does DH reveal itself as critique.

Todd Presner, in an article that argues strenuously for a relocation of digital humanities within the critical tradition of the Frankfurt School, offers a series of projects that supposedly instantiate that tradition. One project Presner endorses (the "Voices of January 25th" and "Voices of February 17th" documentary projects) illustrates "how social technologies like Twitter can be used to give voice to people who were silenced in the 2011 revolutions in Egypt and Libya. Started by John Scott-Railton, a graduate student at UCLA, the projects used Twitter to disseminate suppressed messages from dissidents to the world."[6] Another project (by Xárene Eskandar) "painstakingly documented gunfire, protest sites, photographs, Twitter messages, and YouTube videos, creating a geo-chronology for thousands of reports and media objects that she found online and through networks of contacts."[7]

There can be no doubt that these projects, like Koh's, represent important interventions in terms of content. And though I speak as an American—aware, I hope, of my own position as a citizen of a nation-state that heavily inscribes terms like *revolution, democracy, rebellion,* and *legitimate protest*—I find them moving and inspiring as well. What's more, Presner seeks, at one point, to countenance Liu's charges (which he quotes approvingly earlier in the essay) directly:

The imaginative ability "to make a new move or change the rules of the game" by organizing and "arranging data in a new way," for example, lies at the heart of curation in a cultural-critical mode. It teases out sites of tension and possibility that give voice to particularity and expand notions of participation; it destabilizes and de-ontologizes representational cartographies, corporate platforms, and technologies—not to mention so-called social truths and publicly accepted norms—through new modes of interactivity, memory mapping, consciousness raising, and forms of counter-mapping. One might cavalierly or cynically dismiss this as naive, but I think it embodies the cultural-critical, weakly utopian possibility of the digital humanities. The task, of course, is never finished, and, as such, it demands an ever-renewed alliance between the making practices of the digital humanities and the transformative social praxis of critical theory.[8]

Whether Presner (or, for that matter, this author) is being naive is an open question. We do well to note, though, how easily this paragraph might function as a desideratum for digital art—a mode of expression that presumably need not justify itself exclusively through social action. But the last line of the following passage is the most telling, since it imagines that this alliance is easily made:

While the intellectual origins of critical theory stretch back to embrace elements of the Kantian critiques of reason, ethics, and aesthetics, as well as, perhaps most saliently, Marxist critiques of political economy, we can situate the flourishing of critical theory in the 1930s and 40s with the Frankfurt Institute for Social Research. More than a world view or cosmology, critical theory was a method of dialectical critique for the analysis and transformation of society. Plenty of comprehensive accounts of the Frankfurt

School intellectuals exist, which place them within the cultural-historical context of Germany during the rise of Nazism, American exile in the 40s and 50s, and the resurgence and application of aspects of critical theory within a wide array of disciplinary arenas from debates within postmodernism to possibilities for global democracy. I will not rehearse that history in this short essay, but merely point to some of the key concepts and problematics that, I believe, should inform the cultural-critical function of the "making" in the digital humanities.[9]

Presner declines to rehearse the history of the Frankfurt School, and so will I. Nonetheless, it is hard to imagine any refraction of the Frankfurt School leading toward the kinds of projects Presner praises (to say nothing of DH projects more generally). Certainly, none of the neo-Marxists who created the earliest (explicitly communist) formations of that school in the 1920s could have imagined activist deployment of an instrument of corporate power (to say nothing of a bourgeois "skill" like programming) functioning as an instrument of revolutionary transformation. Nor is it possible to imagine any particular modification of this basic view during the "flourishing" Presner mentions (Horkheimer, Marcuse, Adorno) in the 1930s, in which ideas about the inescapability of cultural forces from above are refined and expanded. To the degree that computation is enlisted in creating the commodities of mass culture (iPhones, Twitter, Facebook, Instagram), it would seem to exclude any possibility of it leading toward what Horkheimer once called "the emancipation of human beings from the circumstances that enslave them."[10] Even if we grant that a phenomenon as variegated as the Frankfurt School cannot be reduced to simple categories and agendas, it remains hard to imagine projects like Scott-Railton's and Eskandar's flowing inexorably from their work. If one were forced to form an alliance between the Frankfurt School—using their insights to reflect upon our own activity—and the projects Presner praises, would we not be forced to concede that the very confusion between "recording" a revolution and participating in one indicates the depths to which rebellion itself has been appropriated, contained, and reified?

The contention is not merely that it is better, all things being equal, for those building things to be theoretically informed by means of the tradition that stretches from Gramsci to Žižek but that failure to do so will have concrete effects on what is built—that without this theoretical background, not just the builders themselves but *that which is built* will be doomed to "ape and extend the technological imaginary as defined by corporate needs and the bottom line through instrumentalized approaches to technology."[11] But what could possibly evince a more thoroughgoing commitment to instrumentalism than the belief that Twitter can be used for good or ill? Earlier in the essay, Presner tries to anticipate the objection that the projects he mentions "were all built on corporate platforms and software" and therefore "inevitably speak their language, surreptitiously mimic their worldviews, and quietly extend the dominance of the technological imaginary as put forward by corporations" (certainly, the objection that the Frankfurt School would have voiced).[12] In a footnote, though, he notes, "they also use open standards, open source code, and free software, such as HTML5, MySQL, and PHP"—as if these tools were not also subject to the same "corporate needs" Presner identifies.[13] It is as if HTML5 were immune from the corporate pressures that continue to dominate the W3C; that the term *open source* wasn't explicitly designed (by Eric Raymond and others) to defang the more ethically utopian vision of "free software" as put forth by Richard Stallman (in an attempt to make it more palatable to companies); as if the copyright and trademark for MySQL, despite the "openness" of its source, wasn't owned by one of the largest multinational corporations in the world; as if PHP's license hadn't been judged incompatible with the GNU Public License by the Free Software Foundation itself. Again, none of these contradictions would have surprised Marcuse.

Another attempt at cultural critique comes less directly through the Frankfurt School and more obviously through the (even less well-defined) cluster of subjects that make up race and gender studies. Tara McPherson's 2012 essay "Why Are the Digital Humanities So White?" (which appears in the *Debates in the Digital Humanities* volume I mentioned earlier) is one example, since it is very obviously a work of critical race studies and at the same time a work that deals explicitly with issues of computation as a form of building and making.

In some quarters, questions like McPherson's are mainly policy matters to be studied from a sociological perspective ("Why are there so few women in STEM fields?"). But for McPherson, a professor of critical studies whose work is mainly focused on race, the most available approach is one that tries to understand localized social problems as standing in some sort of analogical relationship with other historical-cultural movements and artifacts. She therefore turns not to attempts by humanities departments in general or the digital humanities community in particular to attract a more diverse group of students and researchers but to the realization that "the difficulties we encounter in knitting together our discussions of race (or other modes of difference) with our technological productions within the digital humanities (or in our studies of code) are actually an *effect* of the very designs of our technological systems, designs that emerged in post–World War II computational culture."[14] The key assumption here is that power flows outward and downward through historical forces of which we are scarcely aware. We—a localized community of practitioners—are having difficulties because of much larger, hegemonic forces that predate us by decades, if not centuries. We can, however, detect this power, once we realize that "certain modes of racial visibility and knowing coincide or dovetail with specific ways of organizing data."[15]

McPherson begins by giving her readers a highly informed summary of the design principles for which the UNIX operating system is often praised: modularity, simplification, transparency, parsimony, and other features that were felt to aid designers of computational systems in managing complexity. Of particular interest to McPherson is the principle most central to the operation of the UNIX command line—namely, the ability to "decouple" individual functions from one another so as to allow both recombination of activity and containment of error.

Having adroitly summarized the features of a history "well known to code junkies and computer nerds," McPherson then goes on to apply these same terms to another history—one well known "to scholars of culture, of gender, and of race."[16] Almost immediately, the technical terms (some of which were already metaphors) begin to take on an entirely unexpected set of meanings. "The second half [of the twentieth century] increasingly hides its racial '*kernel*,' burying it below a *shell* of neoliberal pluralism"; segregation within the urban center of Detroit mirrors "the programmer's vision of the '*easy removal*' or *containment* of the troubling part"; "across several *registers*, the emerging neoliberal state begins to adopt the Rule of Modularity"; "modularity in software design was meant to decrease 'global complexity' and *cleanly separate* one '*neighbor*' from another."[17]

Though the article is not overtly theoretical, it does depend on a number of theoretical concepts that descend ultimately from the historical materialism of Marx, including Ernst Bloch's notion of simultaneity (which is not mentioned) and Gramsci's notion of "common sense" (which is)—both of which help to form, I think, the ground truth upon which a certain common rhetorical structure in critical theory depends. After all, it is difficult to say how engineering problems on one side of the country are affecting racial politics on the other, unless certain ideas are assumed concerning the nature of historical forces and patterns—particularly when these events are meant not to be taken as analogies but to be taken together as explanations of present reality ("are an *effect* of"). Still, a proviso seems necessary:

> Let me be clear. By drawing analogies between shifting racial and political formations and the emerging structures of computing in the late 1960s, I am not arguing that the programmers creating UNIX at Bell Labs and in Berkeley were *consciously* encoding new modes of racism and racial understanding into digital systems.[18]

Surely not. But the inverse of McPherson's argument seems at least as plausible, if not more intuitive. Why not say that the difficulty in joining discussions of race to our digital productions in digital humanities is not an effect of the design of computational systems but the aftershocks of postwar racial politics? In such a case, we would surely not want to say that those creating racial divisions (or being subjected to them) were consciously encoding new forms of software engineering. The point of this emendation is not to deny any imputation of overt racism on the part of a few engineers at Bell Labs but to make the larger point that actors are, in general, almost never aware of the effect that ideology is having on them (or, for that matter, the effect their ideology is having on others). It is the purpose of criticism to make this implicit set of relationships explicit—to show precisely how ideologies tie command-line butterflies on one side of the matrix to racial hurricanes on the other.

One might ask, though, how digital humanists are to do what technicians at Bell Labs could not? The answer, it seems, is the cultivation of awareness:

The digital humanities and code studies must also take up the questions of culture and meaning that animate so many scholars of race in fields like the new American studies. Likewise, scholars of race must analyze, use, and produce digital forms and not smugly assume that to engage the digital directly is to be complicit with the forces of capitalism. The lack of intellectual generosity across our fields and departments only reinforces the divide-and-conquer mentality that the most dangerous aspects of modularity underwrite. We must develop common languages that link the study of code and culture. We must historicize and politicize code studies. And, because digital media were born as much of the civil rights era as of the cold war era (and of course these eras are one and the same), our investigations must incorporate race from the outset, understanding and theorizing its function as a ghost in the digital machine. This does not mean that we should simply add race to our analysis in a modular way, neatly tacking it on or building digital archives of racial material, but that we must understand and theorize the deep imbrications of race and digital technology even when our objects of analysis (say UNIX or search engines) seem not to be about race at all. This will not be easy.[19]

It is useful to consider the subject positions of all the players in this critical drama. The designers of UNIX and members of racial minorities are acutely aware of certain things but entirely unaware of others. The former undoubtedly thought of themselves as solving a difficult technical problem (systems complexity) with an elegant solution (modularity); the latter were undoubtedly aware that they were themselves being considered a difficult social problem and were being "solved" by being deliberately segregated and partitioned. Neither group, according to a certain way of thinking (not necessarily McPherson's in particular), could see the ways in which they were subject to larger ideological forces, variously described within nineteenth- and twentieth-century theoretical discourse as mind, history, capital, libido, repressive desublimation, desiring machine, and so forth. It is the job of critical race studies to see these very things, and the hope is that this awareness will lead toward some sort of racial comity (or at least, one hopes, to a world in which DH is less white). So while it is true that the designers of UNIX (none of whom were cultural critics) couldn't foresee the wider effect of what they were doing, if they could have seen it, they might have done something else. Or should have. But here, the complexity of the situation reveals itself most clearly.

The problem is that they *couldn't* see it, and the fear is that those humanists who "push the execute button" will join those who can't see—that, indeed, *the very nature of the activity* ensures their ignorance. Uniting critiquing and interpreting with making and building becomes still more urgent: Can one do both? Can one do nuclear physics *and* realize that one has "become Death, destroyer of worlds," or does one form of awareness exclude the other? Vishnu's terrible (and ancient) answer to Arjuna's question is even more disquieting than either choice: Vishnu will plunge into battle—like an inexorable ideological force—with or without the prince. The question of our "complicity" is moot; even if we manage to gain Oppenheimer's awareness, the world will go on without us.

Mark Marino, who is commonly considered the founder of what is now referred to as "critical code studies," brings us closer than anyone we have considered thus far to addressing Liu's objections directly:

> Critical Code Studies (CCS) is an approach that applies critical hermeneutics to the interpretation of computer code, program architecture, and documentation within a socio-historical context. CCS holds that lines of code are not value-neutral and can be analyzed using the theoretical approaches applied to other semiotic systems in addition to particular interpretive methods developed particularly for the discussions of programs. Critical Code Studies follows the work of Critical Legal Studies, in that its practitioners apply critical theory to a functional document (legal document or computer program) to explicate meaning in excess of the document's functionality, critiquing more than merely aesthetics and efficiency. Meaning grows out of the functioning of the code but is not limited to the literal processes the code enacts. Through CCS, practitioners may critique the larger human and computer systems, from the level of the computer to the level of the society in which these code objects circulate and exert influence.[20]

This is precisely what (in Liu's estimation) the digital humanist fails to see: that the objects of building and making "are not value-neutral" and are "more than merely aesthetics and efficiency." Power (culture, interpretation, "larger human systems") is the proper subject of humanistic meditation, and Marino intends to deliver on precisely this aim. The implication, of course, is that cultural criticism is entirely equipped to undertake such study.

In one article, entitled "Disrupting Heteronormative Codes: When Cylons in Slash Goggles Ogle AnnaKournikova," Marino seems to offer a fourth possibility to the trinity of activism, building-as-redress, and self-consciousness: and it is, of all things, art. In the essay, Marino considers the work of two highly conceptual artists: Zach Blas and Julie Levin Russo. Both deal with heteronormativity in various ways (Blas through installations that involve code, Russo more exclusively through inscribed code works).

It is difficult to summarize the work of either artist without quoting lengthy portions of Marino's article; Marino himself surely feels the difficulty of trying to describe works that are situated within specific environments. A few quotes will have to suffice. Of Blas's work:

> Transcoder comes on a DVD. Purple lettering on a black background spells out tC. The C plays off a standard language, such as C. The texts themselves are stored on the disk in a DMG file, much as software might. Unpackaging that volume brings a pink hard drive icon to the Finder menu, again with the tC logo. According to Blas' "about" statement in transCoder, this logo is a visual play on Apple Computer's logo, which for him, calls forth another apple, the poison apple in the suicide of Turing, after his own sexuality was the source of his persecution. Technology, sexuality, repression, and forbidden knowledge ripen the significance of the transCoder apple.
>
> On the disk comes a fictional software development kit (SDK) called transCoder, called a "Queer Programming Anti-Language." "Fictional" is perhaps a misnomer. "Pseudo" fits it better, as in pseudo-code, or mock ups of source code written to sketch out programs for human consideration rather than to execute them on electronic computational systems. The code is not illegitimate because it is "pseudo" but not complete for machine execution or, to put it another way, theoretical. Indeed transCoder is a theoretical software development kit.[21]

Of Russo's "Slash Goggles"—a work that references, in various ways, the fan culture that surrounded the remake of the television series *Battlestar Galactica*—the obvious homoerotic elements (including openly gay characters and homoerotic undertones) are joined to "debate . . . over whether the show disrupts or reinforces traditional gender roles."

> Russo contributes to this conversation in the form of a kind of BSG mod, an imaginary piece of software that allows Cylons to see the sexual subtext of various moments aboard the Battlestar— one that offers a kind of queer vision, subliminal counter- spectator specs.
>
> In her LiveJournal post, partially reprinted in the User's Man- ual, Russo presents the Goggles as though they were a genuine modification script for BioCylons. Russo creates her own fictional user manual, independent of Blas'. In this fragment from it, she offers an introduction, the code itself, and a demonstration of their effects. To illustrate, Russo presents the results in the form of screenshots from the series in which she's added Mad Magazine- style speech and thought bubbles to make explicit the content that is being suppressed. By providing the code and the coding language (which can also be found online), Russo invites readers to interpret the code themselves.[22]

Both works are very obviously forms of critique and attempts at activist resistance. Both works are also explicitly—one might say relentlessly—informed by critical theory. Marino notes of Blas the way the work riffs off the work of Foucault, Donna Haraway, Judith Butler, and Jack Halberstam, and it is obvious that Russo's work is similarly informed: both works abound with "in jokes for theory heads," as Marino puts it. As such, they would seem to fulfill both Presner's and McPherson's qualifications.

But what would an expository work in the humanities look like under the imperatives of art? Could one imagine partisans of distant reading arguing that their charts and graphs are really forms of politi- cal art? If they are designed to critique dominant narratives, it can only be those narratives in which complicity with globalism and neo- liberal ideas are illuminated (i.e., the very awareness that Liu exhorts digital humanists to cultivate) or else the dominance of "critique" as the normative principle of contemporary academic endeavor. If they are informed by critical self-consciousness (a proposition always in doubt, as we saw in McPherson's work), then demands are being made that are not made generally of art itself. Blas and Russo appear to be highly self-conscious artists, but it is difficult to say how and in what way that self-consciousness may be verified. That Michelangelo might have self-consciously worked the image of one of his detractors into the image of Minos in *The Last Judgment* seems clear enough; that the Libyan Sibyls of the Sistine ceiling concretize Michelangelo's sublimated homosexuality presupposes lack of self-consciousness. But we excuse, in all of these cases, such "deficiencies." Authorial intention might once have mattered, but it of necessity contradicts the presuppositions of cultural theory and cultural studies both; artists, like the "masses," are mostly unaware of the forces that act upon them (even, and perhaps especially, when they claim to have such awareness). Indeed, even those explanations that are offered—their insistence on the primacy of the individual as art-maker—only serve to illustrate the inscrutable and sometimes insidious nature of those forces.

In that same article, Marino also considers a piece of software called the AnnaKournikova worm—an irritating, if not particularly novel, computer virus that affected Microsoft Windows users in 2001. In the beginning, the claims are considerably more guarded than McPherson's. The abstract promises only to "interrogate the viral qualities of heterosocial norms"—a more or less conventional critical goal for an essay situating itself within the discourse of cultural studies. Marino reviews the now-famous story of a world-class female athlete and asks, "Is the sexuality of Anna Kournikova the subtext of all of her press coverage or the text itself?"

This question—a question that is fundamentally about culture and how culture works—is then followed by a (mostly) technical explication of the way the AnnaKournikova virus works: its method of encryption, the way it infiltrates the Windows registry, and so forth. What comes next, though, is breathtaking in its leap from object to interpretation—a bringing together of the code's bare artifactual form and its broader cultural meaning that effectively replaces analogy with causation:

Perhaps the most telling moment, the most wormy moment, comes when the code creates a new copy of AnnaKournikova and writes itself into this file. The lines read:

```
Set thisScript = FileSystemObject.opentextfile
(wscript.scriptfullname, a)
thisScriptText = thisScript.readall
```

followed by

```
Set newFile = FileSystemObject.createtextfile
(wscript.scriptfullname, true)
newFile.write thisScriptText
```

The call to "scriptfullname" would return the value "AnnaKournikova.jpg.vbs." Thus, the project first reads itself, then writes itself into a new file. This is the worm's means of replication and where the logic of normative ideologies reemerges. In this way it "replicates exponentially" but systematically, not erratically. (It is, remember, carrying the dominant ideology). In normalized notions, the message or cultural imperatives create a space for themselves in our minds and copy those ideas with always already authority so we can pass them on as naturalized knowledge. If a subject in a society accepts the hail into that society, the hail is inscribed with and inscribes its logic in the mind of the subject, it has already been accepted.[23]

Marino doesn't offer McPherson's disclaimer, but it is hardly necessary to do so. There can be no question of Jan de Wit, the author of the AnnaKournikova worm, having any idea at all that he was replicating the logic of normative ideologies. But the dividing line between good (Blas and Russo) and bad (de Wit) seems to lie precisely in the idea of self-consciousness. If you know you are dealing with heteronormativity—literally implanting ideology in the artifacts you are creating—the result will be good. Do so unwittingly (so to speak), and you run the risk of advancing the agendas of global corporations, creating racial divisions, and maintaining dominant—and necessarily destructive—ideologies.

The implications of Marino's argument are clear: if, while one is building a piece of software in which a series of data-intensive operations are being executed as part of a larger set of simultaneous user events, a debate arises over whether it might be better to pool those operations into a central queue (the building), one must somehow self-consciously bring questions of isolation and community into the realm of the problem. Likewise, if being a gender theorist means that one is considering the ways in which global network forums have served to activate (and sometimes embitter) previously localized debates over the terminology of nonbinary gender identities, one must strive to simultaneously consider that users of these networks experienced less network latency once HTTP/1.1 was released.

I am risking the certain objection that I am being overly flip (and brazenly reductive) in order to further emphasize the difficulties inherent in the exhortations set forth above. Even if the above extremes seem entirely risible, one must also note how easy it would be for the humanist (digital or otherwise) to enact these critical procedures in reverse. Concurrency, it might be argued, appeared in the second decade of the twenty-first century as an urgent technical problem not merely because of the limits of Moore's Law but because global inability to foresee "concurrent" events as intimately related had become a cultural imperative in the wake of 9/11. One might similarly note that while HTTP is a rather dull (if, at the same time, ubiquitous and important) technical standard, it is also one of the numerous sites of negotiation over who "owns" the internet—a subject that takes us quite deeply into the workings of global capitalism and American hegemony. It is likewise easy enough to imagine someone undertaking the projects I just outlined without any serious degree of technical prowess.

Stated in this rough manner, the question that emerges is ultimately whether engaging in one form of activity (building) obligates one to engage in another (the study—or, at least, the awareness—of the potentially destructive effects of power). Joined to this problem is an ethical question concerning whether such awareness is incumbent upon all or only upon those who attach the term *humanist* to their activities (assuming that it is possible for anyone at all). This is not to ask whether one can be a cultural critic while also being a digital humanist, since it is clear that one can; all of the scholars mentioned above have done this successfully, and they are hardly alone. It is also not to ask whether people who build tools can, as individuals, also possess an awareness of the ways in which their actions are or are not imbricated within the structures of power (or culture, or commerce, or entertainment, or the family, or the human psyche). It is rather to ask whether the act of noticing that imbrication is an awareness that (having been suitably enlightened) changes the nature of the activity or whether that act of noticing changes the individual while leaving the activity mostly untouched. The first would serve to utterly racialize (for example) that which would "seem not to be about race at all" (say, building an operating system or designing a microchip). The latter would conceive that awareness as something more akin to what Wittgenstein once called "seeing an aspect"—one may notice that the duck is "also" or "really" a rabbit, though nothing about the image itself has changed.[24] In either case, an explanation of the relationship between building and critiquing that casts the problem as a choice between a bare unreflected instrumentalism and enlightened political awareness commits a kind of category error.

It might, indeed, be a dangerous category error, since it ultimately amounts to an on-the-ground confusion between activism and non-activism. I say nothing philosophically novel in noting that failure to intervene when faced with the suffering of others might be morally reprehensible or that political engagement might be incumbent upon all who possess the franchise (in whatever form). But critical reading strategies do not address these injunctions, and I believe that those who casually assume they do are guilty of a kind of quietism. Reading strategies, at best, might inform and inspire (and even then, only in limited cases) those who seek to make activist interventions in the world. But they are not themselves "activist" interventions in that world. Making and building digital tools is also not easily rectified with political activism (though, ironically, it is a bit easier to imagine "digtal political activism," even if such a thing would be entirely distinct from anything anyone would recognize as digital humanities).

I hope it is obvious that I have not chosen my interlocutors because I regard them as easy targets. To the contrary: the critics and artists I cite above all strike me as making something like "best in class" arguments for their respective positions. And only the strongest will suffice, since Liu's are not the facile dismissals of someone who considers any sort of digital anything to be a kind of existential threat to a supposedly unsullied *Humanitas*. But quietism is at least as bitter a calumny as Taylorism, and those so charged would be within their rights to wonder if, by casting doubt on the possibility of "activist building," I have likewise evacuated reflection, contemplation, and critique of any political meaning at all. And anyway, is it not true that "everything is political"?

In a manner of speaking, I suppose. But as with all categorical imperatives, this one runs the risk of effacing any sort of distinctions at all. In this case, it is the risk of imagining that all acts of "resistance" (Liu's term for what criticism might be) have the same kind of political efficacy—that whether one writes letters to the editor or fabricates letter bombs is really only a difference in degree. Then again, perhaps it is exactly this. In that case, it remains to say where the "standards, protocols, schema, templates, and databases"—and the tools and websites upon which all this relies—stand in relation to a well-theorized conception of "the great postindustrial, neoliberal, corporatist, and globalist flows of information-cum-capital."[25] My contention is merely that they are huddled together far closer on one end of the spectrum than is commonly supposed—that cultural critique within the academy is "political resistance" only in the most elliptical sense.

But this is bad news only if one has already succumbed to the global flows, so to speak. Because in those latitudes, nothing without a clear instrumentalist purpose has any value at all. Even asserting the "utility" of political meaning conforms, ultimately, to the technical, neoliberal meaning of that term—a type of worth or value derived by actors in a system (and not automatically contributed back to that system by those actors). Perhaps it would be better to think not of how "thinking about metadata" might scale into "thinking about power" but of something like the reverse: that our "thinking about power" may, finally, be a kind of technical annotation intended to justify the project of humanistic inquiry to a world wondering what anyone is going "to do with that." Other annotations are possible, and if there is indeed a crisis in the humanities to be discerned in our declining enrollments and evaporation of public support, other annotations may be necessary.

As We May Not Think

The frontispiece to *Museum Wormianum,* first published in Leiden and Amsterdam in 1655, depicts a *Wunderkammer*—a "wonder room" or "cabinet of curiosities" (see Figures 10 and 11). Such rooms were popular among wealthier members of the intellectual elite of sixteenth- and seventeenth-century Europe. They were designed to impress, but they were more fundamentally designed to act as haptic encyclopedias. Key to the Wunderkammer was the often-elaborate system of classification used to organize the room: animal, vegetable, mineral, certainly, but also careful separation of, say, the skeletons of actual animals from the skeletons of mythical animals (also carefully arranged). You would also find numerous human artifacts: ethnographic objects from faraway lands, automatons, compasses, calculation devices. Many historians have pointed out that part of the purpose of these systems of organization was to demonstrate continuity between the natural world and the human world, suggesting, perhaps, that art could not only imitate nature but improve upon it.[1]

But the Wunderkammer was more than a museum. It was meant to be a microcosm not only of the world but of the mind. It contained knowledge, but it more fundamentally represented Knowledge itself. It was meant to reinforce the orderly nature of the universe and (more crucially) the orderly nature of our knowledge about the universe.

The person standing in the Wunderkammer was no doubt meant to be overwhelmed by the objects that literally surrounded them (I don't think I've ever seen a representation of a Wunderkammer that didn't have objects mounted on the ceiling), but at the same time, the Wunderkammer reinforces the overall tractability of the knowledge those objects represent. The person stands, significantly, *at the center.*

Now I'd like to jump ahead (about 350 years) to an infographic from 2010 that depicts what the author terms "the three types of knowledge" (see Figure 12). This appeared in a blog post by Steve

Figure 10. Frontispiece to *Museum Wormianum* (1655) depicting a Wunderkammer. Image courtesy of Welcome Collection.

Figure 11. Engraving from Ferrante Imperato's *Dell'Historia Naturale* (1599) depicting a Wunderkammer. Image courtesy of the University of Erlangen-Nuremberg.

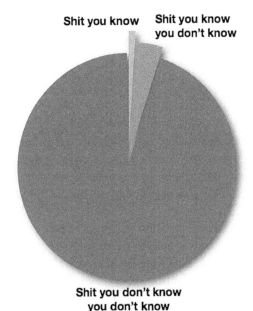

Shit you know   **Shit you know you don't know**

Shit you don't know you don't know

Figure 12. Steve Schwartz's only partly satirical visualization of "the three types of knowledge." Image courtesy of Bridge Global. Steve Schwartz, "No One Knows What the F*** They're Doing (or 'The 3 Types of Knowledge')," Bridge Global, May 13, 2010, https://www.bridge -global.com/blog/3-types -of-knowledge.

Schwartz, who was running a web consultancy in Detroit. It still makes the rounds on tech boards from time to time. The idea goes like this: most of us, upon finding ourselves lost in the woods, would have a sense of what is edible and what is not. An apple, for example, is edible. But what of these unusual berries? Well, you don't know. They could be poisonous. So you move on.

Schwartz asks us to imagine someone who had somehow grown up without this division between the edible and the poisonous. Such a person would march through the forest indiscriminately eating anything and everything that looked edible. And this person would probably not fare well. Schwartz provides another example:

> If I'm an engineer designing a bridge, I know that I need to account for that location's climate when choosing the materials for building the bridge . . . this is stuff I know. I may not know exactly which materials have stress limits within boundaries set by the climate, but I can look it up . . . this is stuff I know that I don't know. However, if I were a veterinarian, and someone asked me to design a bridge, I may not even realize that different materials are affected

differently by environmental factors ... this would be stuff I don't know that I don't know. And in this situation, someone would probably die.[2]

I should mention that all of this appears in a blog post entitled "No One Knows What the F*** They're Doing (or 'The 3 Types of Knowledge')."

Some might recall U.S. Defense Secretary Donald Rumsfeld's reply when asked whether there was any reliable evidence proving that Iraqi president Saddam Hussein was supplying weapons of mass destruction to terrorist groups. Rumsfeld responded by saying:

> As we know, there are known knowns; there are things we know we know. We also know there are known unknowns; that is to say we know there are some things we do not know. But there are also unknown unknowns—the ones we don't know we don't know.[3]

Rumsfeld's statement was subject to quite a bit of ridicule for what seemed to many an obvious bit of obscurantism intended to conceal outright political deceit. For Slavoj Žižek, the quip amounted to evidence of a grave, socially pervasive, and entirely willful form of moral ignorance: "the disavowed beliefs, suppositions and obscene practices we pretend not to know about, even though they form the background of our public values."[4] Far fewer noted that the statement is logically coherent, even if one might ask whether the knowledge of nonknowledge (like Quine's example of the knowledge of nonbeing) might be *some* kind of knowledge.[5] An even smaller number (including, notably, Žižek) asked if there isn't perhaps a fourth category of "unknown knowns"—things we don't know we know and that may approximate something like "tacit knowledge" (even if that is to beg the question somewhat).

This tripart division overlaps with any number of cognitive biases that are difficult to manage (e.g., the illusion of superiority and perhaps also the famed Dunning-Kruger effect). But for Schwartz, people who willfully ignore the third category are literally dangerous. In fact, the whole point of the essay is really to explain why you spend most of your time feeling like a clueless fraud. It's because (God bless you) you have a healthy respect for the third category. In fact, Schwartz would say that our conception of education as adding to the first category (the stock of things we know) is fundamentally flawed. Education, for Schwartz, is not adding to the stock of things we know but rather moving things from the list of things we don't know we don't know into the list of things we know we don't know.

But the question I really want to ask is this: Which representation more accurately represents our present epistemological moment?

It's easy to dismiss the Wunderkammer as offering a naive vision of human centrality and control—a fiction that Schwartz criticizes by making the gnomic category "shit you don't know you don't know" the largest part of the graph (he wryly notes that the graph is not to scale, because "the red slice is unimaginably large"). But in fact, Schwartz's point is to give us back our sense of control by making a virtue of our helplessness. In fact, Schwartz's essay ends with a statement that I would say is every bit as salutary as the *Museum Wormianum*:

> I hope that this helps if you find yourself sometimes feeling conflicted, recognizing the contradiction between your abilities and what other people say about your abilities. When you find yourself in a situation where you don't know what you're doing, don't be afraid to ask for help. Don't ever feel ashamed for not understanding something, even [if] it seems like it should be obvious; if you don't understand it, then it's not obvious, plain and simple.[6]

That quote occurs under the heading "Relax, Be Realistic, You Can Do It"—a motto that would work very well as the sign hanging over the door to the Wunderkammer. It might work as the sign hanging over the modern world (or at least some devout vision of it).

The origins of my field—English literary criticism—are hard to specify; its antecedents go back many centuries, and the process by which it became a recognized discipline distinct from other, cognate endeavors is not at all clear. But Matthew Arnold's writing—his *Essays in Criticism* (1865, 1888) and especially his 1869 book *Culture and Anarchy*—has always held a special, if somewhat anxious, place in the annals of our endeavor. It was in the latter that Arnold defined *culture*:

> The whole scope of the essay is to recommend culture as the great help out of our present difficulties; culture being a pursuit of our total perfection by means of getting to know, on all the matters

which most concern us, the best which has been thought and said in the world, and, through this knowledge, turning a stream of fresh and free thought upon our stock notions and habits, which we now follow staunchly but mechanically, vainly imagining that there is a virtue in following them staunchly which makes up for the mischief of following them mechanically.[7]

If you find that this tugs at your heartstrings—even just a little bit—it's because it is the dream of humanists the world over. The humanities is here imagined as having a therapeutic role. It *helps* us out of our (collective) difficulties by emancipating us from the unexamined life. If you are a humanist, you believe this. There is no way to teach a class in any humanistic subject without assenting—at some level—to Arnold's vision. It is the ground truth of modern humanistic inquiry.

It is also terribly embarrassing and fraught with intolerable difficulties. Who, to start with, is the "we" that forms the subject of so much of what is put forth here? Whose "present difficulties" are we imagining? Matters that most concern whom? The answer, of course, is obvious. Arnold has in mind white, British, educated, wealthy, privileged men. And that surely affects rather profoundly the statement that is at the heart of this quotation: "the best which has been thought and said in the world." Pray, what is best?

I think it is not at all an exaggeration to say that the history of modern humanistic inquiry largely consists in the attempt to reason our way out of this discomfort. Or rather, it is to find some way to describe the humanities as "helping with difficulties" without committing to a narrow vision of either the difficulties or the nature of the help. We have passed through a number of phases with this, and here, the Wunderkammer and Schwartz's graph can help us to understand what those phases might be. Imagine someone (maybe from the present) walking into a Wunderkammer with the intention of correcting its flaws. "Pardon me, sir, but that is not actually the horn of a unicorn; it is merely the helical tusk of a narwhal. And this distinction you're making between animal, vegetable, and mineral, while useful for a game of Twenty Questions, is rather crude. Also, I notice your collection contains no bacteria, despite the fact that bacteria account for a good deal of the biomass on planet earth." You can do this with museums, but also with canons, syllabi, curricula, encyclopedias, and any other guide to knowledge. In English studies, we have spent decades eschewing the notion that some books are better than others and trying to replace it with more inclusive, more representative samples of human culture. It would be hard to regret that effort; we've surely been enriched by the attempt to get it right, or at least get it not so terribly wrong. But none of this questions the basic premise of the Wunderkammer: namely, that it is possible *and desirable* to be representative.

But imagine walking into a Wunderkammer that effectively solved the problem of representativeness by including everything. It doesn't have representative examples of bacteria; it contains every example of every bacterium. It contains every example of everything (the heating and air conditioning bill is quite formidable). It is a one-to-one representation of the universe. It contains, in the words of the Nicene Creed, "all that is seen and unseen."

I submit that your principal desire, upon entering this Wunderkammer, would be to create a collection, far smaller than the original, that presented representative highlights of the vast wonders within. Which is to say, you'd be back at the beginning. But this time, you'd be haunted by a thought that hadn't really occurred to you, despite the fact that you've been standing in this highly inclusive Wunderkammer—colloquially known as the world—all your life. I see stuff I know, and I see stuff I don't know. But what about the stuff I don't know I don't know? Shit.

I hope you'll forgive this fanciful analogy. But as it has no doubt occurred to you by now, I'm really talking about the radical possibility that the humanities now confronts. All books. All paintings. All artifacts. All these things were already in the world; in the case of books, all of them were already in so many libraries through the world. But Google Books—and all similar efforts—strikes us with the possibility that we might actually know what we don't know we don't know.

This is what "big data" actually means. It is neither a matter of grids, and processors, and threads, and mutexes, nor a matter of tera-, peta-, exa-, or any other calculable number of bytes. It is a shorthand for a set of sensations that are, as far as the humanities are concerned, both exciting and frightening. It is both the promise of some kind of revolutionary new capacity (heretofore only crudely imagined in frontispieces of yore) and a provocation leveled against our confidence in the basic premises of Arnold's argument.

Because a world where you don't know what you don't know is

certainly an exciting world, even if it is also a frightening one. That we greet it with such equivocation speaks to our sense of fairness and equanimity (the humane force behind our attempts to get it right) but also threatens to complicate (and perhaps even erase) the methodological rules under which we have operated. I'd like to suggest three things that need to change in a world of big data—three attitudes that we may need to adopt in order to take advantage of the *Überwunderkammern* that are beginning to appear:

Playful Systems

The quest for representation is supposed to be the result of reasoned inquiry into the human record. Forgotten peoples, places, and things must be remembered, and the way to restore that memory is through conscious deliberation and exploration. This is the regime under which we were all trained, and it has worked well. We would be foolish to abandon it. At the same time, 130 million searchable volumes cannot be fully, or even partially, comprehended using ordinary methods.[8] It has been stated many times (particularly of late in various apocalyptic white papers and exegetical grant applications) that no one can read all of that material. But the truth is, even high-performance computers can't read all of that material.

I believe that we're going to have to embrace not just statistics and sampling—the sort of thing text analysis practitioners have been doing for years—but the aleatory and the playful. We're going to stumble onto things. We need systems that trip us.

Heraclitan Systems

The anxiety that has overtaken the humanities is nothing compared to the anxiety that is overtaking libraries. How will we keep track of all of this? ("This" being the Wunderkammer we call the World Wide Web). How will we preserve it? How do we even cite it?

When I listen to such conversations—which are very earnest and very well meaning—it sounds to me as if we are asking the river to stop so we can step in it twice (or perhaps catalog the water molecules for posterity). I would go further (and echo Rich Hickey, the creator of the Clojure programming language) in saying that our obsession with maintaining consistent state awareness in computational systems is about to be a quaint and wholly impractical ideal.[9] We must develop ways to deal with a world of information that does not stop mutating.

Backward Systems

I remember a conversation I had a few years ago with a colleague of mine in the Computer Science Department. I was telling him about an idea I had that involved directed graphs and characters in novels. I have done some work with graphs and networks as a way of visualizing narrative structures, and I wanted to see if we could apply machine learning algorithms to the broad classes of graph structures I was detecting.

My colleague kept asking me, "What are you looking for?" I spent about forty-five minutes trying to say something that didn't sound like, "I don't know! I'll know it when I see it! I'm looking for something cool! Something interesting!" But the truth is, that is exactly what I was doing. I was uncomfortable saying that, because it's backward. In the sciences, you're supposed to develop a hypothesis and then go test it—developing any necessary processes or instruments in light of the questions you're investigating. You're not supposed to invent the microscope and say, "Hey, let's look at this strand of hair. Maybe we'll see something" (though that is undoubtedly exactly what its early inventors did).

The trouble is this: any problem you can state is by definition outside of the realm of what you don't know you don't know. One way to get at that stuff is to invert this process completely. Develop a tool or a technique and then go think of something interesting to do with it. We need to be open to this not as an accident that we retrospectively claim as part of our methodology (a bit of revisionist history that I suspect is all too common) but as a first-class methodology that can put us in a position to see something new.

Discussions about big data—and especially about high-performance computing in the humanities—often highlight the mismatch between what the humanists know and what the computationalists know. And it is right that we acknowledge this mismatch and try to alleviate it to the degree that we can. I always walk away feeling impressed by how quickly the computationalists are able to intuit what is interesting about humanistic problems and to think with us about methodology in creative ways. I also know (from the looks on their faces) that the computationalists are often surprised to learn how often we are guided mainly by intuition and anecdote. But really, this is not the disconnect that should concern us. The disconnect that should concern us is that between the dominant methodologies to which we both subscribe and the changing nature of the artifacts we both propose to illuminate. That is the challenge, and it will require not a technical revolution but a philosophical revolution. In fact, it is why "digital humanities" may eventually come to represent not a mashup of two disciplines but a recharged and rejuvenated version of both.

Learning to Code

I got into digital humanities for the money.

That will come as a dispiriting revelation to scholars like Alan Liu, who have accused digital humanists of failing to reflect on the ways in which the digital humanities "advances, channels, or resists to-day's great postindustrial, neoliberal, corporate, and global flows of information-cum-capital."[1] Yet it is a simple fact of my intellectual life that I got into digital humanities because I was broke.

I was in graduate school during the 1990s and, like all graduate students, had submitted to that voluntary state of semipoverty that accompanies the pursuit of a PhD in English. I was at the University of Virginia, and a job was posted for a part-time position at the Electronic Text Center. That seemed preferable to my other avocation (as a very unarmed security guard). What I didn't realize is that I was walking into the World Wide Web.

The Electronic Text Center—now moribund as an organization but fully alive in the collection that resulted—isn't mentioned as often as it might be in the casual and conflicting histories we tell about the rise of the digital humanities, but it had a profound effect on my own development as a scholar. Its brief could not have been simpler: create a searchable digital archive of . . . well, everything. As with the earlier and more famous Project Gutenberg, the "what" of it all seemed far less important than the "why."

The Electronic Text Center ("Etext," as we called it) thought of itself as a more mature and expert version of Project Gutenberg. Michael Hart—the man who had essentially invented the e-book—had chosen editions and recensions willy-nilly. Etext would accession its texts according to the best rules of textual criticism, with particular emphasis on provenance. Both Hart and our group were intending, like Joseph, to open the granaries to those starved for the artifacts of human culture. Anyone with a computer would be able to access anything from Aeschylus to Zweig (and we were confident that that would one day mean *everyone*). We, with more than a hint of self-satisfaction, were opening the doors a bit more carefully.

It would be hard to understate the giddy naivete that permeated our efforts. Hart's decision to name his project after the inventor of the printing press says it all, or most of it. We were standing at a unique pivot point in world history. Before, you would need to travel to the British Library and present your academic credentials (and your damn good reason) for examining the *Beowulf* manuscript—a text for which we have precisely one extant copy. Now anyone could read it! One of my earliest memories of contact with this new world is of me sitting next to a senior medievalist scholar as we waited—endlessly—for a high-resolution copy of a single page from one of the manuscripts of *Piers Plowman* to appear on the screen of a Solaris workstation. Once we had it, we both thrilled to the way in which you could drill down to the pockmarks on the vellum. A bit confounded, I remarked that it was almost as good as the real thing. "Stephen," he said with resigned pleasure, "It's better than the real thing."

How different this bright-eyed world was to the English Department just on the other side of Jefferson's Academical Village. There, I was being trained in the hermeneutics of suspicion—trained to look precisely for the outworkings of power in human cultural artifacts exactly as Liu would suggest. But here in the digital scriptorium, that prime directive of contemporary scholarship was held in strange abeyance. No one, including me, was attempting to flee the theoretical or the critical; we could easily have made the right noises about suspicion and contingency to anyone who asked. But in practice, we were as wide-eyed as children.

My own particular role in the august task of Changing Everything, it must be said, was rather minor; I was engaged in that slightly exalted form of data entry known as SGML tagging—placing angle brackets around paragraphs, dialogue, quotations, and as many other structural features of a text as time would permit. At some point, the job of assistant director of the Etext Center opened up, and I committed the ultimate heresy of taking a full-time job while still in graduate school. The email I received from the graduate chair strongly resembled that of an abbot trying to discourage a contemplative monk from pursuing the active life of a wandering mendicant; I would hardly be fulfilled by forsaking Derrida for data. But I liked the work, and I had suitably absurd notions about my ability to complete a dissertation quickly while working full time.

That new job was mostly administrative. I had to make sure that the work was doled out properly and that everyone was paid, attend to incoming "unadorned" text, and generally help to oversee the operation. I loved it, of course. I was, after all, part of a revolution. Tagging, though, is for the birds (at least the kind that I was doing); only revolutionary fervor (or the promise of pin money) could compel one to spend hour upon hour determining the beginnings and ends of paragraphs. The thought occurred to me that perhaps some of this could be automated. And isn't *programming* the way you automate things? And isn't C a programming language?

I had spent most of my life thinking that only geniuses could program. My dad, after all, could program, and he was clearly a genius. I, on the other hand . . .

My father started as an hourly factory worker at Polaroid in the midsixties. He had grown up on a dairy farm in eastern Massachusetts, and that had convinced him (to my grandfather's horror) that there was absolutely no way he was going to work on a farm for the rest of his life. And so, after a brief stint in the army, he landed the job at Polaroid. Making $1.89 an hour.

College had never been in his future. His family couldn't afford it, and they were suspicious of the whole thing anyway. After a few years at Polaroid, he became a supervisor of some sort (with a salary!), and that probably seemed to him about as far as his "career" (a word he probably wouldn't have used) was going to go. But Polaroid had started a co-op program that would allow workers to go get an undergraduate degree while working part time at a reduced salary. Now, they weren't going to pay for a degree in English literature or history (which is probably what he would have gone for, if he'd had the opportunity). But Polaroid would pay for an engineering degree. So he signed up to major in computer science at Northeastern University. He was thirty-one years old.

So right from the start, computers were connected in my mind with social mobility (a term *I* certainly wouldn't have used). As a kid, I watched my father struggle through the standard curriculum for engineering (physics, calculus, statistics, chemistry), and it all seemed to me to be impossibly difficult. But that also made it seem heroic.

And I was *definitely* going to college. My mother grew up on another farm (in Ireland), and one of the constant background narratives of my childhood had been that she had come to this country "to have educated children."

There was, though, the problem of the eldest son (me) being about the worst student imaginable. I was a complete disaster right up until the twelfth grade—your classic slacker who "doesn't apply himself," but I was also disorganized and unable to focus on anything. So I grew up with very romantic ideas about what college was all about, and about what computing was all about, but also with the clear sense that my ability to be part of this narrative was very much in question. My parents' certainty that I would be one of the educated children gradually gave way to the thought that I might not be able to get into college at all.

In 1981, around the time he got out of school, my father bought one of the very first IBM PCs. This was an expensive thing—really beyond what he could afford at the time—but he managed to justify it, because computers had become integral to his career at that point, and he felt like having one of these would push his career further forward. I was immediately entranced by it, but not for any of the reasons my father was. It came with lots and lots of manuals in ring binders, nearly all of which had to do with programming. And really, what else would you do with a computer that, at least by today's standards, barely seemed to have an operating system? The answer to that question seemed obvious to me. The other thing you did was play games on it (and I knew that, because we were always going to computer stores in the Boston area, and they were selling titles like *Adventure* and *Apple Panic*). I was all over that.

One hears stories of people—who are now highly skilled professional engineers—learning to code back in the 1980s on machines like the Commodore 64, the Atari 800, and the TRS-80. They wistfully describe combing through the pages of *Byte* magazine (each issue of which was nearly half the size of the Sears catalog) looking for "code listings" that they could copy (by hand) to their own systems. Shuttered in their bedrooms for hours, they pored over the meager documentation for the BASIC programming language, creating little text-based games, making the computer play short segments of music, and even venturing into graphics (and, for some intrepid souls, assembly). Some now deliver solemn "back in my day" sermons about how they "started from nothing" and lecture us about the rigors of 8-bit computing.

It has been pointed out that anyone whose family could afford a computer in those days was living in a highly privileged environment, and that is certainly true. What, then, shall we say of me? My family had a computer that made the aforementioned systems look like pocket calculators. Since I imagine that there is nothing more dull and tedious for those without benefit of such privileges to be subjected to anxious confessions of those who do, I will simply mention the irony of this.

I said I had been the worst possible student in high school, and I exaggerate not at all. I repeatedly failed any subject that involved numbers, but really, I performed poorly in any class that involved studying (or thinking of any kind). There were, however, two exceptions: English and typing. English never seemed like "studying" at all (reading stories and poems?), and while I wouldn't have admitted it to my friends, I was falling seriously in love not just with the stories but with the whole subject. And as for typing: I could tell my own wistful stories of learning to type in an ancient typing lab on an old manual typewriter. It did, however, have the happy result of making me, to this day, the fastest typist I know. So there was never any question of what I would major in when I (to my parents' complete astonishment) got into college. I declared as an English major at the first opportunity, on the assumption that this was the only way I was going to survive.

During my first semester, I took a class with some very grand title (The Role of the Citizen in the West, or something like that) taught by a professor of political science. It was a two-part course that explored this question with Plato, Aeschylus, Machiavelli, Augustine, and then later with de Tocqueville, *The Federalist Papers,* Weber, and various others. I was smitten. Perhaps I had just managed to mature enough to have the discipline to actually read these things, but part of it was the professor himself. He acted as if the questions we were considering were the only ones worth thinking about, and he lectured with a kind of hypomanic intensity that was entirely new to me. Truth is, I wanted to talk like him, and think like him, and I wanted to have discussions like the ones we were having for the rest of my life. I told my friends that I thought *The Oresteia* was the greatest thing ever written (as if I had read enough to form an opinion on the matter). I might have switched to classics right then and there, but I knew that would mean learning ancient Greek, and I had failed French. And that was only a subset of the larger problem. I wanted to stay in college forever, and my track record suggested that I might not survive the first year. Still, fear is a strong motivator, and I managed to acquit myself quite well in college. Four years later, I graduated with a degree in English.

Some years later, I am in graduate school having an experience that feels a lot like one I'd had before. I couldn't have been fifty pages into Brian Kernighan and Dennis Ritchie's classic *The C Programming Language* before I knew that my whole scholarly direction was about to change (I had been studying to be a theater historian). Putting text online was all well and good, but—and I was surely the only one in the world who had had this thought—the real revolution would come once those texts were in machine-readable form and could be manipulated and analyzed with code. I was barely through wrapping my head around while loops before I realized that it was the text morphed, transformed, and visualized that was going to change my discipline forever. I was, once again, smitten.

So smitten that I proceeded to learn half a dozen programming languages in the space of a few years, along with relational databases, design patterns, functional programming, and discrete mathematics (the last of these with the help of a brilliant professor who kindly agreed to tutor me). Some of this overzealousness was born of my worry that I would never be taken seriously as a technologist, since my only formal training consisted of English degrees. But deep down, I felt no different than I had entering college. I'm just not the sort of person who succeeds at this sort of thing. Impostor syndrome is the psychic commonality of everyone in graduate school; I felt like the spy who knows their cover is already blown.

I want to be very clear (before I go any further) about the moral of this story, which is not that if a dunce like me could learn to code, then anyone can. It is not even to say that amor vincit omnia, and that with *timor* and labor at your side you can do just about anything. It is certainly not to boast of my own successes. But there are elements of this story that bear on the shibboleth of "coding" in the digital humanities, the anxieties it produces in many, and on various misconceptions about what programming actually entails. And I consider myself an expert on this subject, because (as I intend to demonstrate) most of the ways I went about it were entirely wrongheaded.

I must confess to having drawn a few of these "false morals" myself over the years. For a long time, I really did believe that anyone can learn to code (I do still believe something like that, but for an entirely different set of reasons). I suppose I also bought into the highly questionable notion that "grit"—a capitalist keyword if ever there was one—was the key to achieving anything. I am far more skeptical of that notion today. And while I'm proud of my successes, I am far more likely to see the role of luck and privilege than personal brilliance and gritty determination.

The very first mistake I made was imagining that only "geniuses" can learn to code. That might seem obviously wrong, but I had a very particular kind of genius in mind: namely, people who were good at math. Having repeatedly failed algebra in high school, I knew that I was excluded from that group. I held to this notion even after finishing my first book on C, despite the fact that there is precious little math in that book, or really in any introductory book on programming of which I am aware. But while I suspected that the math would come later (and finish off my attempts at learning the subject in one fatal blow), I think the trouble was that I thought the skills—or the "habits of mind"—of a programmer are the same as those of a mathematician. And on this point, I was dead wrong.

At some level, computation is all about mathematics. I still occasionally hear discussions of "binary logic" or "zeros and ones" as the root of computation—usually offered as some kind of hard limit to what computers can do and thus a matter of great consolation for those who are worried they might one day be replaced by them. But this really isn't a particularly foundational matter. It is entirely possible to create not only computers based on different number bases (10, 16, 60 . . .) but "analog computers" that do not use discrete states at all. The latter, rather than creating a generation of sentient computers bent on enslaving humanity, were almost entirely obsolete (with a few minor exceptions) by the 1960s. The fact that nearly all computers are "binary" today is mostly the result of practical considerations— more a matter of efficient electrical engineering than anything else. We would do better to say that the root of computing is the ability to perform mathematical computations and to store and retrieve the results of those computations. The limits of computation are therefore quite literally the limits (and the possibilities) of mathematics. That is, ultimately, the root of the computer's awesome power and the hard limit of what it can do.

But in practice—which is to say, from the perspective of the programmer—computation is only as mathematical as the problem you are attempting to solve. If the goal is to model the aerodynamics of an aircraft wing, the programmer's problem naturally becomes extremely mathematical; if it is to dynamically generate a website, there will likely be no mathematics involved at all. And most computational problems—even dazzlingly complex ones—look more like the latter than the former. What's more, in either case, the "habits of mind" that are the most essential look the same in both cases.

I celebrate with great fanfare the moment when my students successfully print "Hello, world!" to the screen. "Today," I say with great solemnity, "you have become programmers." "Hello, world!" is, after all, not only a program but perhaps the most famous program of all time, and they just wrote it themselves. But the truth is that they actually become programmers a few minutes later when I ask them what would make the "Hello, world!" program better. "Well," they say, "perhaps it could greet you by name?" Or, "Maybe it could greet you in your chosen language." "Maybe it could say 'hello' to something chosen at random ('hello, chair')." But how do we do any of that? That exercise immediately addresses the two hardest things about programming, which are (in order): figuring out what to build and designing the solution.

Figuring out what to build is, by far, the most difficult matter, and analogies with work in the humanities abound. The trouble with writing expository prose, after all, does not lie with the quotidian matter of putting coherent sentences together, or knowing how to use commas, or the possessive, or semicolons. The main problem is having something to say. Ideally, we want to say something new or modify or expand an existing idea. Once we have that (ferociously difficult) problem solved, we then face the fearsome challenge of trying to "design" an argument. "What goes where" (as we all know) is not about the commas. If penetrating philosophical meditation were a matter of syntax, we'd all be quite a bit more productive.

The analogy strengthens with the first homework assignment I give my students. By the time I assign it (usually after the first class) they know enough programming to write a Mad Libs program (a program that prompts the user with questions and then prints out a story with the user's words inserted into it). My requirements for how such a program should behave are intentionally vague; "Pray, make it funny" is about as specific as I ever get. From a programming standpoint, the problem is so simple that I cannot recall anyone ever passing in a Mad Libs program that didn't work. They are rightfully proud of that fact and usually assume that we're done. They are therefore bemused and mystified when I proceed to savage their work with mirthful abandon for the next hour.

"'Enter a noun': You're rather throwing us into the pool, Tom. It's true that I did just type the command 'madlibs,' but what if I don't know how to play?" "Oh, wait. Carmen, you have a 'Welcome to Mad Libs!' That's good. And Lisa, you have not only 'Welcome to Mad Libs' but also some instructions. That seems even better. But I suppose we have people who know how to play and some who don't. Should it be optional?" "Yes, we could do a 'press H for help,' but is there a way to split the difference? Something that's maybe welcoming like Carmen's *and* has optional help?" "'Enter a noun.' 'Enter a verb.' 'Enter a *gerund*?' Wait! I'm nine years old! What the hell is a gerund?" "Well, if a gerund is a word that ends in *-ing*, then . . . maybe: 'Enter a word that ends in *-ing*?' But honestly, I'm still wondering about that word *enter*. I don't know. Is that right? Should it be *type*?" (One year, I taught the class to a group of aspiring computational linguists and got "Enter a modal verb.")

Inevitably, someone decides to write an obscene Mad Libs program. "Folks, this is a kids' game. And while your blue joke is mildly amusing, do we really want a seven-year-old grappling with, 'Enter a sex organ'? And how, exactly, do we exclude kids? Ask their age? They'll catch on to that one fast. Is there another way to do it? Is this an interface issue, or is it about sequestering the program itself? And by the way, you'll have to try a lot harder to embarrass a lit professor." "What do you say, class? As punishment, perhaps we'll have him write a limerick generator (where obscenity is more or less a requirement of the genre). "Okay, but actually, that's a much harder problem. What makes it harder?" "That's right. We'd need to find words that rhyme, *and* we'd need to count syllables. And there's a third thing: we'd have to know not only where the stress falls in a word but where the stress could be *forced* to fall. What? Yeah, I don't know either."

"Enter a noun. Enter a verb. Enter a fruit. Enter a type of car. Enter a body part. Enter an adjective. Enter the name of a city. Enter a noun. Enter a verb. I'll be honest, Nick; I'm losing the will to live. When does this end?" "But look! Lakshmi put in all these 'You're doing great! Only five more to go!' It's like a progress bar, which is actually not quite as exact a science as it might appear. And isn't it funny? What happens when a program seems to stop doing anything, but there's *no* progress bar? What? Right. Me too. I wonder if the program is broken."

They all fail the assignment. I give them all As.

Because this, in miniature, is what's really hard about programming, and it's a challenge that appears not only in the interface but in the code itself. In later assignments, I keep asking them whether any future coder will be able to understand what this function does. Or why these three functions aren't abstracted into one function that can do triple duty. But then, would doing that make it *less* readable? The function itself might not be very complex. It might confuse not because of *what* it does but because of *where* it does it. How do I make it so the main logic of the program is clearly over here and more ancillary (but still necessary) operations are over there? Audience, accessibility, and privacy (only a few of the ethical dimensions of "what to build") appear in less obvious ways in the way we structure code and make it available to others but are no less critical. And many of these issues show up even in the simplest things we build.

What are the habits of mind that one needs in order to succeed at this? I never asked my students how much math they know, but early on, I used to give a quiz asking them what technologies they are familiar with (with a few obscure acronyms thrown in to root out the "sandbaggers" who already know how to program). Today, that "quiz" looks very different. One of the skills is the ability to look at a complex problem or task and think up a radically simplified version of it (sort of the way one tries out a simplified version of a piano piece or maybe focuses on the right hand first). Another requisite skill is the ability to figure out the right order in which to do things (sort of the way a chef reads a recipe and then sets up their mise en place using little "hacks" learned along the way to simplify the process). Yet another skill is the ability to remain aware of a complicated set of "rules" and know which ones are hard and fast, which ones can be bent, and which ones might be more like "house rules." "Anyone play an instrument? Clarinet in middle school? Perfect! Anyone like to cook? Anyone like games and puzzles? Don't worry; it doesn't have to be Go or Contract Bridge. Dungeons and Dragons might be even better."

But again, the most requisite skill of all, and a natural corollary of the "what to build?" question, is the ability to discern a need and communicate a solution to that need (using a very broad definition of *need*). And I'll just say it: students in the humanities are better equipped than most to tackle that one. I am not at all surprised (though still delighted) when students say, "I can't believe I'm good at this!" I can.

I understood none of this when I started out. I mentioned that I engaged the services of a tutor in discrete mathematics early on. I had somehow arrived at the conclusion that everyone who knows how to program also knows this subject, and therefore I must know it. The person who came to my rescue was a computer science professor by the name of Worthy Martin (there's a name to conjure with), who was, at the time, one of the codirectors of the Institute for Advanced Technology in the Humanities. By that time I had, with a combination of truth and lies about my abilities, landed a job there as a full-time programmer.

How to describe Worthy . . . Worthy is one of those computer scientists who wonders why anyone would want to spoil the beauty and elegance of computation by getting involved with *actual computers.* That is to say, he was as pure a theoretician as you're likely to find in the already rarefied discipline of computer science. I was, it turns out, making another false assumption about programming. I suppose I imagined (stating the case a bit extremely) that computer scientists were the ultimate black-belt programmers and that computer science was largely about building things. Neither thing is true, and in fact, I suspect that though Worthy might have once learned to program, I eventually came to understand that it would not be wise to trust him with any part of the actual production code I was writing (though on the matter of what to build and how to design it, he did indeed have his black belt). He didn't correct my impression that discrete mathematics was an essential subject, but I now realize that he had immediately figured out what I was actually asking him to teach me: not a set of skills but a certain way of thinking; not an injection of knowledge about a subject but a dose of confidence in my abilities.

"Discrete mathematics" is not a methodology for exploring a class of mathematical problems in the same way that calculus and linear algebra are, but the designation for a set of topics loosely united by the fact that they deal with "discrete" (roughly, "countable") mathematical objects—as opposed to the "continuous" mathematics (something like, "things that vary smoothly") with which these latter subjects deal. Traditionally, it includes graph theory, combinatorics, topology, number theory, and set theory, though most of these topics can be studied in isolation. Since computation is mostly about "discrete" things, it's usually a required course for computer science majors (and in fact, the term itself appears to have arisen as the designation for "support courses" first offered to computer science students sometime in the 1980s). Years later, I studied certain elements of the subject more systematically (and only because I was facing the humanities equivalent of an "aircraft wing" problem). Worthy's presentation, by contrast, was entirely unsystematic. It was something like a greatest hits album of important results in the field. We went over the traveling salesman problem and Cantor's diagonalization theorem (the "proof" for the existence of transfinite numbers), explored the properties of finite sets, and did a bit of mathematical logic. Or rather, we went over a series of random paradoxes over which Worthy probably still loses sleep.

But Worthy wasn't trying to teach me "discrete mathematics." He was trying to show me how to break complicated things that we don't understand into smaller things that we do and build back up from there. He was trying to show me that even though a demonstration might be compelling, it might not be entirely "satisfying" (which is to say, it might not actually settle the matter, because the "design" is flawed). He was trying to show me what an "abstraction" actually is and why abstracting a problem into the intellectual ether might actually serve to make the concrete, practical problem in front of you clearer. And finally, he was trying to show me that I wasn't "bad at math." Having now been a programmer for twenty-five years (or so), I can say with confidence that I have rarely used any of the actual mathematics I learned from him. I use the habits of mind every day, but mathematics isn't the only area in which one can acquire those habits. It is no accident that discrete mathematics is one of the world's prime sources for games and puzzles, and anyone studying game mechanics is already putting themselves through a version of the same curriculum.

I am, to this day, very grateful for the tutorial and very grateful to the tutor (who was doing the whole thing pro bono). But my certainty that I needed to understand this subject was part of a deeper flaw in my approach to programming. Everything about my education to that point had convinced me that if something looks anything like a skill, the proper approach is to learn the skill and then go use it. That's more or less the way it works with typing, after all, and it felt like the way it works with learning foreign languages. You learn to type, and then you go type. You take classes in German, and then you know German. I knew that learning something like eighteenth-century literature wasn't quite like that, but perhaps I had some vague notion that it was. More than one professor in grad school interpreted a youthful swagger I regrettably seemed to possess with an exaggerated sense of my own expertise. They were wrong about that; I was truly terrified by my dark past as a terrible student. But I was wrong too. I had a deeply flawed sense of what "expertise" actually is.

I mentioned earlier that I had "learned half a dozen programming languages in the space of a few years," but of course, I had done nothing of the sort. What's worse, I thought I had, because I equated reading books on programming and writing a few toy programs with "knowing" the language. The truth was that I no more "knew C" after reading the "K&R" than I would know Italian after glancing at a few verb tables. Today, I do know C quite well, but that brings me back to the Mad Libs program.

One year, a student wrote a Mad Libs program to the utter delight of her two brothers (aged five and seven, if I recall). Since they liked it so much, she spent the rest of the semester writing what is—without doubt—the most sophisticated Mad Libs program ever written. It began with interface customizations but eventually led her into customized output based on which brother was playing (and to the Flesch-Kincaid readability formula). That, in turn, presented a number of at times formidable design problems, which, again, were not so much about the difficulty of the algorithm as the tractability of the design. Each new thing she learned in class resulted in new features in the Mad Libs program, but more importantly, she found herself having to go off the syllabus to learn aspects of the language and its third-party libraries that weren't part of the course at all. By the time she was done, the program was coming up on two thousand lines of code (far in excess of any line count necessary for the toy problems they were assigned).

And that established a rule in my programming classes forever more. "The minute you have an idea for a 'real' program—something you'd actually like to exist in the world, because it solves a problem you have or addresses someone else's need—come talk to me. I may well exempt you from all future problem sets." The reasons for this "alternate track" are manifold. A student writing a "real program" will learn more about programming than I or anyone else could ever teach them. They almost always remain highly motivated to finish it, because they really do want the program to exist. There might be two little siblings clamoring for more, or it might be that the code alleviates an annoyance in their actual lives ("scratching an itch," as we say in programming circles). Most of all, it reinforces a lesson I am desperate to communicate to them any way I can: namely, that a computer is not a machine in the same way that a plow, or a clock, or even a printing press is a machine. It is a machine for creating other machines. As a result, nothing about their computational world should be thought of as "given" from above (by Apple, Google, Facebook) and therefore immutable (even if those same companies are desperate to have you think otherwise). Anything can be changed. Anything can be reimagined. And the set of things no one has thought of yet is effectively infinite.

But it communicates another lesson too, and that is that in practical terms, no one ever really "learns programming" and then writes software. The process is not only intensely iterative but also "just-in-time" (to borrow a metaphor from the arcane world of compilers). We learn what we need to know as we need it, and the "we" here is all programmers, no matter how experienced. Sometime around week four or five, class morale starts to dip. It is at that point that I give a speech something like the following: "I know that you're all feeling a bit incompetent, and since none of you are incompetent, this is probably a very uncomfortable sensation. But I have been programming for a long time, and I can tell you that this feeling is permanent. It will never go away. I learned the topic of today's lesson by beating my head against the keyboard. I despaired over my ability to ever understand it. Now it seems easy and effortless to me. But when I'm done here, I'm going to go back to my office to work on a problem that has *me* feeling incompetent, and once I figure it out—and I will—I'll just move onto the next moment of incompetence. Our only hope, then, is to get comfortable with feeling incompetent, to remember that education is about what we *don't yet know,* and to try to help each other when we can." A few weeks later, when the lesson of that day now seems blazingly obvious (and they are wondering why they ever struggled with it), I remind them of that "week four" feeling.

I hope the story I'm telling here is ennobling and encouraging. But I would be remiss if I didn't mention another thing I understood not at all when I started and that I now understand (if only secondhand) with poignant clarity.

I am very proud to have taught hundreds of students to program. I have sometimes taught in computer science programs, but I have more often taught it (sometimes carefully hidden from the eyes of curriculum committees) in English departments. Most of those latter classes have been majority women—a proportion so beyond the most extravagant dreams of gender parity in computer science as to be nearly unimaginable. That, of course, has nothing to do with any particular approach I take to the subject but with the simple fact that English programs tend to have slight majorities of women enrolled. Be that as it may, when some of these students say, "I can't believe I'm good at this," there's an extra dimension to their sense of surprise.

And some of the women I have taught are very good at it indeed. I mentioned "beating my head against the keyboard" while trying to learn to program. But every year, I have students (often women who are encountering the subject for the first time) who cock their heads slightly as I draw on the whiteboard, appear to have complete and instant understanding, and then go off and write programs that are dazzlingly well conceived and perfectly designed. They are, in other words, natural engineers who are certainly better at this than I was at the same stage, and they will probably go on to be better at it than I will ever be. I often take such students aside and (at the risk of betraying my own discipline) suggest that they might want to take a more advanced class in the Computer Science Department.

Often, they do just that. A very small number go on to major in it, and some are now professional engineers with advanced degrees in the subject. But that is hardly the common case. I am far more likely to encounter them a year or so later, and when I ask how it went, they tell me that "it just wasn't for them." "Was it too hard?" (I already know the answer to that question; it certainly was not.) "No, it wasn't that." "Well, was the professor not welcoming and encouraging?" "Oh no, he seemed overly so" (it is always a "he"). As the conversation proceeds, it becomes incandescently clear that what was bothering them was the fact that they were one of the few women in the class and that they were being sent subtle (or not so subtle) signals that they didn't quite belong. They don't always find the word they're looking for to describe it, but the word is *culture*. And that culture stops most of them dead in their tracks.

Many years ago, I had one of these extraordinarily gifted students in my class. She was a first-year student who not only excelled at programming but had also managed to land a spot on the graphic design team for the university newspaper (a rare thing for someone in their first year). Her designs in my class (on both the front and back ends of the code) were at times breathtakingly elegant, and I was always telling her so. At some point in the semester, the Computer Science Department had announced a contest for the best smartphone app, and I immediately encouraged her to sign up. She demurred, saying she didn't know enough for something like that, but since she was also the shy and retiring sort, I began to wonder if she was nervous about going to the meeting. "Well, what if I go with you to the orientation meeting? If it's not your thing, it's not your thing. But what if it is?" So off we went together at the appointed time to the "kickoff meeting."

I don't think either of us were particularly surprised to see a large room full of men (there were a few women in attendance, though none of the people leading the meeting were women). And they had helpfully provided pizza. That, though, was about the only thing that was "thoughtful" about the gathering. The entire presentation was a flurry of football metaphors and porn jokes—a farrago of masculinized "geek speak" and bro culture. Everything about it seemed calculated to convince my poor student that she had wandered into the wrong locker room. I suppose I had some sort of teaching moment on my hands as we walked back from the meeting together, but I was too boiling with fury at my colleagues to offer anything useful (I think I was wondering whether it would be possible to sue an entire discipline for sexual harassment). When I finally did calm down enough to stammer something about it, she looked at me as if I had just arrived on planet earth. What else did I expect?

It certainly wasn't the first time I had become aware of such phenomena. I had seen it firsthand many times. And though I am coming dangerously close again to tedious confessions, I have to admit that something about that event revealed to me the sheer moral ineptitude of the situation in a way I hadn't quite grasped before. It is true that I expected more from *them,* but I couldn't really avoid the fact that "them" also included me. "Geek culture," after all, had by that point in my life become *my* culture as well. It's not enough to think of oneself as "not like the other boys" while at the same time being one of the boys. I patted myself on the back for not giving lectures laced with toxic masculinity, but hadn't I participated in this kind of event countless times? It was really only the vision of the crestfallen student next to me that had shaken me up. Or rather, the fact that she was visibly *not* crestfallen. For her it was the same old humiliating nonsense.

I wish I had easy answers to these problems (which extend, of course, to racial and ethnic minorities as well). I have occasionally entertained the idea of writing an editorial for the flagship journal of the Association for Computing Machinery or the Institute of Electrical and Electronics Engineers in which I offer the modest proposal that we teach all computer science classes in humanities departments, where I sincerely believe the culture is less toxic. I can only say that I am tired of the hand-wringing about women in STEM and particularly tired of the "leaky pipe" metaphor (the idea that we send the message that STEM isn't for girls early on and that it slowly and imperceptibly builds up from kindergarten to college). I'm tired of it not because it's wrong but because it often seems meant to absolve those of us at the end of the pipe from doing anything substantive to stop it. But then, reforming the systemic problems of a "culture" is not an easy problem.

Still, we know what to do on those rare occasions when a student has clearly managed to learn to "hate poetry" at the feet of a middle-school teacher. We know what to do when our students come to us knowing quite literally nothing about the subject at hand (and rejoice to hear something like, "I can't believe I like political science!"). We know very well when lack of self-confidence is the real root of a student's difficulties. And we also know—or should know—how to create welcoming, inclusive environments in our classes. If we don't, it is our own professional failure that is causing the problem. And unlike my moment of accidental feminism years ago, we are now supported by numerous groups that are working very hard to plug the holes earlier in the pipeline.

I said earlier that the two hardest things about programming are knowing what to build and knowing how to design a solution. But neither observation directly addresses what is hard about *learning* to code. The story of my gifted, thwarted student is an extreme case, and it is one that in important ways affects only those who labor under the additional burdens of racism, sexism, and other forms of bigotry. But I believe it throws into sharp relief some version of the difficulty we all face. People *on the other side of a PhD* worry that they aren't smart enough to learn to program. We are beset by old wounds and the vagaries of venturing into intellectual cultures and communities that we perceive as alien to our own. We shudder at the thought of adding another dimension to our own strangely persistent sense of impostor syndrome. We don't want to go back to feeling incompetent all the time (even though most of us still feel that way trying to navigate the twists and turns of our own specialties). I have often wondered, though, whether diving into the unknown as often as we are able might make us better teachers in the end. That's one reason a lifelong humanist might learn to code; it's also a reason why a computer scientist might want to learn how to engage in scholarly discussions of Shakespeare.

Should *you* learn to code? I've made some ineptly stated comments on that subject in the past and have spent a good deal of time trying to rephrase them ever since.[2] But let me approach that question from a few different angles in light of what I've written above.

I teach programming at least once a year, but I spend most of my time as an English professor teaching theater history. I do not read Norwegian (Ibsen) or Swedish (Strindberg) and have only a tourist's knowledge of Russian (Chekhov), though I teach plays translated from these languages every semester. Should I learn Norwegian? The answer to that is "perhaps." I'd feel nervous about venturing forth with professional scholarship on Ibsen without it, and the day may come when I decide to take that dive. But surely there's no reason for me to learn Occitan; I am not a medievalist, and I have no intention of becoming one. Then again, I am grateful to have studied ancient Greek. It comes in handy when I'm teaching ancient theater, but to be honest, it's not something I "use" very often. Survey your own intellectual inventory, and you'll find similar bits of "useless" knowledge. You've probably tried to minimize those and maximize other things (less American history, more French theory; fewer articles, more monographs; less contemporary fiction, more eighteenth-century drama). We order most of our scholarly journeys this way—doing something like "just-in-time" evaluation of what we need to move forward with what we're studying.

Programming is really no different. There are vast regions of digital humanities where writing software is not really the principal requirement (though there is often some technical facility—equally as challenging—that *is* required). There are other areas where the matter seems far more pressing. But how much programming does one need to know? Will "tourist Python" do, or does one need to embark on the (effectively impossible) task of "mastering" C++? The best advice I can offer is to do with programming what we do with everything else: figure out what will move your scholarship forward and go from there. It's possible that someone else can write what you need, but if you are truly in possession of that most rare and precious thing in programming (an idea about what to build), it might be the case that the ideal candidate for that task is you.

It would be wise to remember, though, that we only rarely present our own subjects in terms of practical need. Why learn Occitan? Because some of the loveliest poetry ever written was done so in what (I am told) is a remarkably subtle and supple language, and our world broadens every time we learn anything. I bristle slightly whenever I hear programming described as a "useful skill," because I know it also as a stirring intellectual exercise. I marvel daily at the things others have written, and I lose myself for hours trying to create something that is utile dulci—a little machine in which the useful and the beautiful are inextricably joined and arise from one another. Those who know Occitan (and can one ever really *know* it?) might sometimes feel that the rest of us are missing out. And we are, of course.

But the real intellectual peril lies with neither of these extremes—neither in the exigencies of time and necessity nor in the rapturous climes of art for art's sake. The tragedy would be failing to move our intellectual stories forward because we have convinced ourselves that we cannot for reasons that have nothing to do with aptitude, interest, availability, or necessity (obstacles that can range, as I hope I have demonstrated, from the personal to the sociocultural). If I often make a plea for programming in particular, it is only because I know to do what all teachers know to do. I would like to be the sort of teacher who invites people into my intellectual world not with demands and shame but with generosity and encouragement. I would also like to be the sort of scholar that heeds the exhortations of other people's journeys.

So: Learn to program only if absolutely necessary. Learn to program for no other reason than curiosity. And never go into anything for the money.

Stanley and Me

In December 2011, Stanley Fish started publishing a series of online essays for the *New York Times* on digital humanities.[1] To summarize: he doesn't like it so much. And for those of us who like it a great deal, this was a curious mixture of good and bad news. It was bad news, because being publicly attacked by an extremely eminent public intellectual in the paper of record is a bit terrifying for scholars who already spend a good deal of time defending themselves in far less public venues. It was good news, though, because being attacked by a gray old man in the gray lady is exactly the sort of thing that tends to set our vast network in motion. Despite our much-vaunted newness, the digital humanities community, in its online form, resembles nothing so much as the scholarly discourse of sixty or seventy years ago. Back then, it was not uncommon to see attacks and parries playing out across several numbers of a journal, as so-and-so offered a response to Professor So-and-so's late comments on Hopkins's use of accentual meter. The Republic of Posts tends to do exactly this when digital humanists all around the world are reading the same thing on the same day—a phenomenon that happens very often online and almost never off it. What's more, Fish was naming names: friends of ours, books of ours, ideas we found compelling, and doctrines we held in common. Really, this was going to be ever so much fun.

But then he did something that ruined the whole thing for me in a stroke. In the midst of this mighty Oedipal struggle, he called me "perhaps the most sophisticated theorist of the burgeoning field" and proceeded to comment on my work at some length and with a good deal of charity.[2] He doesn't like what I'm saying either, really, but—well, actually, it was hard to tell. He seemed to appreciate my work, or find it provocative . . . or something. Maybe he *did* like it?

"Damn it," I thought, "What am I supposed to do now?" Suddenly, it seemed churlish to jump into the fray. I'll admit to a certain guilty pleasure in having my work characterized by a famous scholar as "so-phisticated," but for the most part, I felt embarrassed by the whole thing. It would have been far easier to join those who had lately been skewered by the great Stanley Fish, because (as was obvious to every-one I know) they had all been treated unfairly. When this sort of thing happens, digital humanists tend to eschew the detached ironies of our more theory-obsessed forebears; our favorite rhetorical mode is something like righteous indignation tinged with self-deprecating humor. But I, having dodged a bullet in all of this, really had no cause for indignation of any kind. So in my flummoxed state, I decided to say nothing. I wrote a few tweets—mostly in response to a torrent of good-natured ribbing from far-flung colleagues and friends—and let the whole thing go on without me.

I'm already sounding a bit too grand and self-absorbed about all of this, so let me allay any fears you might have. I'm not about to give My Belated Response to Stanley Fish. I'm not going to provide some kind of witty (read, pompous) refutation of his arguments, defense of my friends' arguments, or anything like that. I do, however, want to toss around a question that I have been thinking about for a long time and that the Fish affair brought into sharp relief. Can you have compu-tational text analysis and literary criticism at the same time? To get at that, we have to go back a bit.

Back when I started being a digital humanist—sometime in the midnineties—almost everyone I knew in the then-as-now "burgeon-ing" field was interested in the World Wide Web. *Hypertext* was the bold and exciting term on everyone's lips, and there was much effu-sive talk of a new democratization of scholarship. I was as enthusiastic about that as everyone else, but I had managed to become entirely enthralled with a much older form of geekery. I had fallen in love with programming languages, and like a hammer looking for a nail, I was casting around for ways to use that in the study of literature. That led me to the quite considerable (and already decades-old) body of schol-arship surrounding what was then called "computational stylometry."

It's important to remember that back then, text analysis had noth-ing of the sheen it has now. I hope I won't offend anyone who might have participated in this pioneering phase by saying that the field of text analysis was, at that time, a bit of a backwater even within the barely noticed field of humanities computing. Not many people were doing this sort of thing, and the ones who were tended to form a very narrow, if passionate, band of enthusiasts. Nonetheless, I think I can fairly say that I devoured every article written on the subject from Busa to that point and was completely enchanted by the whole thing.

Still, I found myself experiencing the same moments of doubt that were even then being expressed among text analysis practitioners. Most disquieting for me were those moments in which stylometrists pointed, somewhat sheepishly, at the areas in which they felt their algorithms dare not tread. John Burrows and Hugh Craig, in one of the most stirring technical articles in the field at that time, had used principal component analysis to distinguish Romantic from Renaissance drama. After reading that article, I became convinced that such methods could lead to entirely new ways of thinking about periodization, gender, language, genre, cultural change, and much else. But in the midst of unfolding their marvelous mechanism, they casually averred that the sort of explanations offered by George Steiner—who had located the shift from Renaissance to Romantic drama in the loss of a "redemptive world-view"—were "well beyond the ambit of present computational stylistics."[3]

I was mostly able to quiet my discomfort with this sort of disavowal. Perhaps it was only "beyond the ambit" because the whole thing was still burgeoning? It struck me that there was basic research that needed to be done on text analytical methodologies, and much that needed to be theorized as well. Being a graduate student at the time, it even seemed possible that I was destined to boldly amble where no one had ambled before. There *was* a way to connect word-frequency lists to redemptive worldviews; we just needed to figure it all out.

Then I read an attack on the work of Louis T. Milic by a scholar named Stanley Fish.

I don't hear Milic referred to very often in digital humanities these days, but he was at least as important a pioneer as Roberto Busa or John Burrows. His 1967 book, entitled *A Quantitative Approach to the Style of Jonathan Swift,* is, as far as I can tell, the first book to tackle specifically literary-critical questions using computers. I had encountered him many times in my attempt to read everything I could about computational methods in literary study—particularly since he was the author of over fifty scholarly articles. Milic died in 2003 (the year I got my PhD).

Fish's attack was entitled "What Is Stylistics and Why Are They Saying Such Terrible Things about It?" (which is, of course, the second chapter of Fish's highly influential 1982 book, *Is There a Text in This Class?*). I've never been exactly sure who was saying terrible things about stylistics at the time, but it seemed to me absolutely clear that no one was saying anything as terrible as what Fish was saying. Fish's most recent attack on digital humanities is mild by comparison.

Milic's work mostly involved word-frequency analysis; Fish was entirely interested in interpretation. So when Milic asks, toward the end of his study of Swift, "What interpretive inferences can be drawn from this material?" Fish is eager to hear the answer.[4] And Milic's answer is this: "The low frequency of initial determiners, taken together with the high frequency of initial connectives, makes [Swift] a writer who likes transitions and made much of connectives."[5] Here's what Fish had to say about that:

> As the reader will no doubt have noticed, the two halves of this sentence present the same information in slightly different terms, even though its rhetoric suggests that something has been explained. . . . There is, in short, no gain in understanding; the procedure has been executed, but it hasn't gotten you anywhere. Stylisticians, however, are *determined* to get somewhere, and exactly where they are determined to get is indicated by Milic's next sentence: "[Swift's] use of series argues [that is, is a sign of or means] a fertile and well stocked mind." Here, the procedure is not circular, but arbitrary.[6]

Milic, in other words, is made to look ridiculous (rather than the quite gifted scholar he certainly was). But when I read that passage, I found myself confronting an awkward truth about computational methods in literary study. For while Milic's was an extreme example, it nonetheless brought forth an uncomfortable feeling I had about it. Text analysis very often consisted of the attempt to enlist sophisticated computational methods in the service of banality. Literary text analysis, in other words, was failing at its most essential task; it wasn't generating *literary criticism*. The question for me became as explicit as this: Could we have a computational stylometry that made Stanley Fish happy?

A moment ago, I cited Burrows's contention that George Steiner's observations were "well beyond the ambit of present computational stylistics." We should pause to consider precisely what it is that lies beyond. Allow me to quote some Steiner (from his 1961 book *The Death of Tragedy*):

> The tragic personage is broken by forces which can neither be fully understood nor overcome by rational means. . . . Where the causes of disaster are temporal, where the conflict can be resolved through technical or social means, we may have serious drama, but not tragedy. More pliant divorce laws could not alter the fate of Agamemnon; social psychiatry is no answer to *Oedipus*. But saner economic relations or better plumbing *can* resolve some of the graver crises in the dramas of Ibsen. The distinction should be borne sharply in mind. Tragedy is irreparable. . . . To ask of the gods why Oedipus should have been chosen for agony or why Macbeth should have met the Witches on his path, is to ask for reason and justification from the voiceless night. There is no answer. Why should there be? If there was, we would be dealing with just or unjust suffering, as do parables and cautionary tales, not with tragedy. And beyond the tragic, there lies no "happy ending" in some other dimension of place or time. The wounds are not healed and the broken spirit is not mended. In the norm of tragedy, there can be no compensation.[7]

George Steiner has been praised as a polyglot polymath and decried as a Eurocentric blowhard. But I will gladly say that whatever else Steiner was, he was a gifted literary critic—someone who, ideally, employs gorgeous writing in the service of profound observations about human culture. If this is the thing that is "beyond the ambit," then why bother? Can any of us really say that we have seen this kind of thing—or anything remotely like it—arise from the quantitative analysis of literary texts? I'm quoting Steiner only because Burrows did; pick any literary or cultural critic you like and ask if you've ever seen an explication that arose from the workings of an algorithm get anywhere near it. I don't mean algorithms generating beautiful and provocative critical prose; I mean algorithms leading the critic toward the sort of thing that literary critics want to say about human culture and its artifacts.

But even as Fish was exposing this rather embarrassing weakness, he was at the same time (somewhat inadvertently) showing us the way out. Fish's real problem with computational stylometry in general (and Milic's work in particular) is that nothing in the "machinery Milic cranks up" authorizes the leap from data to interpretation. And when nothing authorizes the leap, you can leap anywhere you like. Fish again:

> One might conclude, for example, that Swift's use of series argues the presence of the contiguity disorder described by Roman Jakobson in *The Fundamentals of Language*; or that Swift's use of series argues an unwillingness to finish his sentences; or that Swift's use of series argues an anal-retentive personality; or that Swift's use of series argues a nominalist rather than a realist philosophy and is therefore evidence of a mind insufficiently stocked with abstract ideas.[8]

My observation concerning that sarcastic list of interpretative possibilities is this: every single one of those would be great. A text analytical argument that went in any of those directions would represent a momentous breakthrough for digital scholarship. Someone needs to write an article in which they use Levenshtein minimal-edit distance and naive Bayesian inference to show that Jonathan Swift had an anal-retentive personality. I would never cease praising any critic who undertook such a task.

The reason we don't do that, of course, is because we feel as if "nothing licenses" that kind of leap—just as Fish noted. To the degree that text analysis depends on scientific methods of measurement and evaluation, we might say the license at least *feels* more restrictive than usual. But what licenses Steiner's leap? What licenses any leap? The text? Of course not. But why must "the data" adhere to a requirement that we long ago disavowed for text? Why can't data function within the same interpretative regime—and fulfill the same hermeneutical functions—as text? Text sometimes operates in the service of objectivity and empiricism, but sometimes not (in the humanities, we might say almost never). Might the same be true of data? Is there a humanistic way to generate and understand data that licenses the kind of leaps we want to make?

Fish, in the end, was unable to imagine a hermeneutics that admitted neither of license nor constraint. I suspect he's right about some system of license and constraint being necessary for meaning, though his notion of "interpretive communities" always struck as a bit too simple a description of what is undoubtedly a much more complex, multivariate phenomenon (Wittgenstein, I suspect, gets us closer to a robust description of how meaning is "constrained").

But let us return once again to beautiful literary criticism. Consider the following work by another very skilled literary critic:

> Halfway through "Areopagitica" (1644), his celebration of freedom of publication, John Milton observes that the Presbyterian ministers who once complained of being censored by Episcopalian bishops have now become censors themselves. Indeed, he declares, when it comes to exercising a "tyranny over learning," there is no difference between the two: "Bishops and Presbyters are the same to us both name and thing." That is, not only are they acting similarly; their names are suspiciously alike.
>
> In both names the prominent consonants are "b" and "p" and they form a chiasmic pattern: the initial consonant in "bishops" is "b"; "p" is the prominent consonant in the second syllable; the initial consonant in "presbyters" is "p" and "b" is strongly voiced at the beginning of the second syllable. The pattern of the consonants is the formal vehicle of the substantive argument, the argument that what is asserted to be different is really, if you look closely, the same. That argument is reinforced by the phonological fact that "b" and "p" are almost identical. Both are "bilabial plosives" (a class of only two members), sounds produced when the flow of air from the vocal tract is stopped by closing the lips.
>
> . . . In the sentences that follow the declaration of equivalence, "b's" and "p's" proliferate in a veritable orgy of alliteration and consonance.
>
> Even without the pointing provided by syntax, the dance of the "b's" and "p's" carries a message, and that message is made explicit when Milton reminds the presbyters that their own "late arguments . . . against the Prelats" should tell them that the effort to block free expression "meets for the most part with an event utterly opposite to the end which it drives at." The stressed word in this climactic sentence is "opposite." Can it be an accident that a word signifying difference has two "p's" facing and mirroring each other across the weak divide of a syllable break? Opposite superficially, but internally, where it counts, the same.[9]

I am quoting (and I hope you'll forgive me for doing so at some length) from the famous broadside that occasioned these remarks: Stanley Fish's final piece in the *New York Times*.

Am I alone in thinking that this is lovely? I am aware of how problematic this is, given that Fish is using his interpretation of Milton to mount an argument for why digital humanists are deluded. Perhaps I should say that I like this *kind* of thing—a reading that takes us from the large to the small and back again. Meaning requires, among other things, an act of faith on the part of the reader, and in another context, I might well take the words of a famous Miltonist (like Fish) as evidence that he believes his own reading and thinks that I should believe it as well. I would hope to walk away with a deeper understanding of Milton and of the theologico-orthographical currents of the seventeenth century. There were lots of blog posts written in the wake of Fish's articles. The most famous of them, though, was Mark Liberman's post entitled "The 'Dance of the P's and B's': Truth or Noise?," which I can summarize as easily as I summarized Fish's article at the start of this essay: Liberman thinks Fish's reading is bullshit.

In the second part of Fish's attack on stylometry, he says that "proponents of stylistics literally don't know what they're doing," but that's hardly a charge that will hold against Liberman.[10] Liberman is able to establish beyond any doubt whatsoever that Fish's "veritable orgy of consonance and alliteration" is, statistically speaking, more like a kiss on the cheek. After several paragraphs interspersed with graphs showing local distributions of bilabial plosivity, Liberman concludes that "a trivial application of statistical methods, humanistic or not, suggests that his idea is probably 'false,' 'noise,' and 'mere play.'" He then asks, "Have I missed something?"

I don't know how to answer that, exactly, but I am absolutely certain that *I* have missed something. Fish's reading is literary criticism without data; Liberman's is data without literary criticism. Neither one seems to me exactly right. I cannot imagine literary criticism—or, indeed, any variety of humanistic discussion—flourishing under the constraint of having to prove its observations using statistical methods prior to advancing any claims. I also can't imagine every attempt to use computational methods resulting in critical flights of discipline-defining significance.

But here's one thing that I think makes either project impossible:

the belief that the only hermeneutically legitimate procedure is one that moves from interpretative judgment to evidence. Here's Fish:

> I began with a substantive interpretive proposition—Milton believes that those who suffered under the tyrannical censorship of episcopal priests have turned into their oppressors despite apparent differences in worship and church structure—and, within the guiding light, indeed searchlight, of that proposition I noticed a pattern that could, I thought, be correlated with it. I then elaborated the correlation.
>
> The direction of my inferences is critical: first the interpretive hypothesis and then the formal pattern, which attains the status of noticeability only because an interpretation already in place is picking it out.
>
> The direction is the reverse in the digital humanities.[11]

I said I wasn't going to give my response to Fish, but here I must: This is complete and total nonsense. I hope I've made clear my admiration for Professor Fish's work and its influence on my own thinking, because I cannot resist noting that on this issue, Fish literally doesn't know what he's talking about.

The idea that criticism only happens when you proceed from interpretative propositions to supportive patterns is, at best, a rhetorical dodge: "I had a very grand thought, and lo! I found it in the text." To say that patterns cannot urge us toward interpretative propositions is to deny the text any serious role in the process of cognition. Has Fish never noticed a pattern and *then* had a thought about it? Is nothing perplexing in Milton? Is there nothing that reveals itself as a pattern but without clear resolution or meaning? Prior interpretations undoubtedly define in advance the regime of our noticings (the elaboration of that idea is one of Fish's greatest contributions to theoretical discourse), but surely that is not absolute. Otherwise, every interpretation would succeed by force of will (or force of narrow-mindedness). Surely the text's ability to surprise us with noticed, but unresolved, pattern is not only one of the great pleasures of the text but the source of a great deal of its power.

I doubt very much if Fish would disagree with my critique as stated, but if one concedes that reading is a process whereby patterns urge interpretations and interpretations bring forth patterns (there is no "natural" sequence or direction here), then we are halfway to saying why you might want to generate a computational program from a critical question *or* generate an interpretation from a computational procedure. Why not do both? In fact, why not do both within tight, concentric loops of reading, hacking, thinking, and interpreting? In order to do this, we have to resist both of the apparent constraints that present themselves. A literary criticism that can only advance claims that are shown to be empirically valid is as deadening to the project of the humanities as a computational activity for which humanistic discourse lies permanently beyond its ambit. Risks need to be taken in both cases. In the former, the risk of saying something humanistically true but empirically false; in the latter case, of saying something empirically true that is humanistically false.

At the end of his essay, Fish states (with a certain resignation) that "whatever vision of the digital humanities is proclaimed, it will have little place for the likes of me and for the kind of criticism I practice."[12] I cannot really believe that that's true, since my own thoughts on text analysis—which have very often been considered seditious by other text analysis practitioners—have their roots in another critic's prescient, if brutal, attacks on the very thing that has held me in thrall for the better part of twenty-five years.

Stanley and me? We go way back.

Data Mining

Mining data. The word evokes images of pickaxes and front-end load-
ers, or else rakish Indiana Jones types gamely hefting golden trea-
sures from the otherwise unremarkable sands. The literary-critical
equivalent, one presumes, involves making similar excavations into
the undifferentiated fields of textuality—the "words, words, words"
of the burdened and overwhelmed reader—in the hope of finding . . .

Well, what exactly? I have many times suggested "pattern" as the
treasure sought by humanistic inquiry: which is to say, an order, a regu-
larity, a connection, a resonance. I continue to insist that this is, in the
end, what humanists in general, and literary critics in particular, are
always looking for, whether they're New Critics, New Historicists,
New Atheists, new faculty, or New Englanders. Pattern is the linchpin
of all humanistic argumentation from the Platonic dialogues to the
Dialogic Imagination. Whether conceived as metaphysical reality or
as desiring machine, pattern is the raw material of the hermeneutics
of the disciplines usually designated among the humanities.

This would be a banal observation—as unenlightening and tauto-
logical as saying "everything is political" or "everything is text"—were
it not for the fact that (like these worn phrases, once upon a time) it
encourages us to see a connection that might otherwise be obscured.
For if humanistic inquiry is about pattern, then it isn't completely
crazy to suggest that computers might be useful tools for humanistic
inquiry. Because long before computation is about YouTube or Twitter or Google, it is about pattern transduction.

The words we use to describe what we're doing reinforce this connection. Woolf *reconceives* gender identity; Hurston *reimagines* the
interplay of race and place; Moretti usefully *reconfigures* the English
novel. We likewise ask our students to notice, to see, to find, and ultimately (we hope) to "re-" as we do.

But not to *mine* and *excavate,* precisely. We dig *Hamlet,* naturally,

and we'd of course like them to dig it as well, but we do not present
the task of literary criticism or historiography as the process of finding
some intact but buried object beneath the surface. That's because we
have for a very long time now conceived of the patterns we're looking
for not as "out there" but as "in here"—not as preexisting ontological
formations but as emergent textual epiphenomena. Someone might
discover a new planet, but anyone who says they have "discovered"
the origins of Situationism or the Roman Empire is (we hope) speaking metaphorically.

My purpose in saying all of this is not to suggest that we get rid of
terms like *data mining, media archaeology,* and similar locutions but
only to point out that all such terms are threatened with metaphor
shear. *Metaphor shear,* you'll recall, is that incomparable term coined
by Neal Stephenson to describe the experience of using Microsoft
Word:

> Anyone who uses a word processor for very long inevitably has
> the experience of putting hours of work into a long document
> and then losing it because the computer crashes or the power
> goes out. Until the moment that it disappears from the screen, the
> document seems every bit as solid and real as if it had been typed
> out in ink on paper. But in the next moment, without warning,
> it is completely and irretrievably gone, as if it had never existed.
> The user is left with a feeling of disorientation (to say nothing of
> annoyance) stemming from a kind of metaphor shear—you realize
> that you've been living and thinking inside of a metaphor that is
> essentially bogus.[1]

Metaphor shear, we should notice, is not the dispiriting revelation
of the man behind the curtain. Neither is it that sudden release from
a trance one experiences when the fire alarm goes off in a theater or
we miss our stop because of a novel. Metaphor shear is a moment of
exasperated surprise born of an entirely incorrect notion about what
is actually happening. Not "It's only a movie!" but rather "Wait. This
isn't a movie?"

And so it is with *mining.* When I started in digital humanities, being a text analysis practitioner was something like being a devoted
student of Byzantine sigillography or of the history of Miaphysitism.
No one really cared (or, for that matter, understood) what we were

doing, but we loved what we were doing, and the small but solidly international group of practitioners was enthusiastic and supportive. None of us could have imagined jobs in the area, articles in the *New York Times* about what we were doing, buzz at the MLA about data mining, or "n-gram" as a trending topic on Twitter. None of us would have dared to dream of an Office of Digital Humanities at the NEH giving actual money to people like us.

But then text analysis sort of arrived. That came about in part because of the general rise of the internet, the creation of large-scale text archives like Google Books, and the rebranding of artificial intelligence as the provably useful and occasionally astonishing task of "machine learning." Could the marvels of the latter have implications for humanistic study? People began reading our articles, inviting us to give talks, asking us to write books. Really, life could not have been better for someone like me who would rather write software and stare at columns of words and numbers all day than do just about anything else. But no sooner had we arrived than people started asking us a question that we were perhaps less than forthcoming about with each other: Where are the *results*?

It's not that text analysis practitioners don't use that term; we use it all the time. We also use terms like *hypothesis* and *control group* and *data point* and *method* and *success* and *fail*. Many of us are even guilty of describing ourselves as "mining." But as with Microsoft Word, the metaphor is essentially bogus. It's bogus even when we say it's not. And that's because when we're doing it right, the whole thing reveals itself to be "humanism as usual."

To work with text is not automatically to be so engaged. Scientists studying the human genome are working with lots of text, as are marketers looking for ways to sell motor oil. We might even say that they are looking for pattern, but, to radically abuse Bateson's phrase, therein lies the difference that makes a difference. To search the human genome for a pattern that might indicate a genetic component to type 2 diabetes is to search for a specific thing that we would very much like to find. The marketers are looking for something that correlates with purchases of motor oil. When they find it ("it" being anything from potato chips to bath towels), they'll immediately use it to their advantage.

What are humanistic miners looking for? Several years ago, the NEH began a grant program called Digging into Data. One project it funded was called "Digging into Image Data to Answer Authorship-Related Questions." What do "authorship-related questions" involve? You know, "finding salient characteristics of artists."[2] Another, called "Digging into the Enlightenment," proposed to discover "how the spread of ideas at the global scale relates to the dynamical processes that operate at the local scale."[3] Yet another, the laconically entitled "Harvesting Speech Datasets for Linguistic Research on the Web," sought to "evaluate theories about the form and meaning of prosody."[4] No one working on the human genome—or, for that matter, the motor oil–ome—would tolerate the vague and imprecise language here employed. How will they know that the characteristics are "salient?" And where is the null hypothesis in their search for the interactions between the global and the local? How many theories about the "meaning of prosody" do you suppose they'll discover to be irrefutably false?

Perhaps I seem to ridicule these projects. I don't mean to. If anything, I mean to suggest their clear alliance with the grandest traditions of humanistic inquiry. Every project gleefully proclaims itself to be "digging into data," but on closer inspection, it becomes clear that they aren't digging even in the metaphorical sense. They are, instead, doing something more akin to the meandering *parole* of the literature or history classroom: asking questions, suggesting answers, reading, pondering. The astonishing thing isn't, in the end, the ways in which high-performance computing and "big data" transform the humanities; rather, it is how much of the hermeneutical basis of humanistic inquiry—the character of its discourse and the eternal tentativeness of its "results"—remains invariant. The revolution is not hermeneutical so much as methodological.

Which is not to say that it is any less a revolution. In fact, it might be more revolutionary than anything that has happened in humanistic study in fifty years, precisely because the traditional humanities disciplines are so radically (if you'll pardon me) undermethodologized. And that's precisely why we need to remind ourselves from time to time that our metaphors are just that.

This is made harder than it should be by the fact that disciplines (and, just as often, companies) unconcerned and in some cases unfamiliar with the terms of humanistic discourse had the privilege of naming the animals. It's hard to imagine even the most positivistic of the old nineteenth-century philologists referring to what they did as "mining," and yet what could be more natural to an engineer? But even if we are unable to change the language of what we do, we can remind ourselves that just because the language is borrowed from another discourse does not mean that it now has the same meaning it once did. Indeed, the still-nascent discourse we call "digital humanities" might be most precisely defined as the attempt to figure out what that new meaning is.

Centers of Attention

I've been involved with digital humanities centers for over twenty years and have now held most of the positions that one can hold within them (short of actually directing one). I've been a kind of intern, a graduate student staff member, a full-time software engineer, an outside consultant, and a fellow. I've watched centers rise and fall, flourish and fade, but centers have always played a, well, central role in my scholarly life. What have I concluded from this long involvement? I've concluded that centers are people.

Now, that's a bad way to begin, because in addition to a rather unfortunate association with *Soylent Green,* it also suggests any number of coarse platitudes and bromides. "It's really about the people," we say—mainly as a way to thank them when it seems appropriate to do so or to emphasize that whatever terrifying bureaucracies might arise, this is still all about human beings and collaborations among them. It's the sort of sentiment companies emblazon on T-shirts and coffee mugs. It's the mantra of departments that, despite their avowed commitment to people, continue to go by the degrading and dehumanizing title of Human Resources. But I don't wish to ridicule the notion too much, because as far as humanities research centers go, this really is the one thing needful. And yet I rarely see efforts to create centers that proceed from the proposition that centers are about people.

I've spoken with many people over the years who are either trying to create a center or raise the profile of an existing one. Centers, it seems to them, are exactly how you "get into digital humanities." I often hear resigned comments from faculty at other institutions who "don't have a center," weary and nervous confessions from those who are "working on getting a center," and delighted cries of jubilation from people who finally, at long last, "have a center." And I'm often invited to act as a consultant for groups at one or another stage of this process.

They invariably want to talk about money, and computers, and infrastructure—about the balance between research and service, the various reporting lines, the projects they might undertake, their position relative to other centers, grant funding, outreach, and furniture. Often, they are brought up short when I ask a question that seems to me a very logical one to ask (especially for a group that hopes to be "all about people"): Who here is doing digital humanities? The answers are breathtaking. "Well, there are some people around who we think would be interested, but we haven't really contacted them yet," or "You know, it's really spread across a few different departments, and we're hoping to use the center to bring them together." Sometimes the answer is, "Um, us" ("us" being the two or three people to whom I posed the question). The credo, in other words, is that if we build it, they will come. And while the movie from which that line comes is admittedly less risible than *Soylent Green*, the belief that having a server, a set of cubicles, and a sign will create that community is every bit as fatuous as the belief that if you create a baseball diamond, the 1919 White Sox will emerge from the surrounding cornfield.

Some stories regarding the formation of digital humanities centers are deceptive in this regard. One of my favorite founding stories involves the Institute for Advanced Technology in the Humanities (IATH) at the University of Virginia, where a lot of my ideas about centers were formed. According to the story, IBM offered to donate a server to the University of Virginia (this was back when such things were a lot rarer and a lot more expensive). The university naturally approached the Computer Science Department asking if they'd like the equipment. The Computer Science Department, amazingly, said, "No." They had heard, however, that there were some people over in English and history who were doing things with computers. Maybe ask them.

It's easy to imagine this server washing up on the shores of the College of Arts and Sciences and starting a strange cargo cult among a group of people who normally didn't work with each other very much. There's a guy in history who's into computers, and there's someone in English. Neither of them really knows what they're doing, and the computer science people are too busy with serious computational matters to help out the poets. The librarians, fortunately, know more than the computer scientists about how to actually maintain a rack server, and so they get involved. Questions arise: Where do we put this thing? Who pays for its upkeep? Doesn't it need, like, maintenance or administration or something? And are we really qualified to design websites, given that none of us have the faintest idea how to draw? That this turned into one of the most vibrant centers of intellectual activity in the field—a hugely influential research group that would be widely imitated—should surprise no one.

We like to marvel at the technological wonders that proceed from things like servers, but in this case—I would say, in all cases—the miracle of "computers in the humanities" is the way it forced a certain subset of a highly balkanized academy into new kinds of social formations. Anyone involved with any of these big centers will tell you that they are rare sites of genuine collaboration and intellectual synergy—that they explode disciplinary boundaries and even (occasionally) the cherished hierarchies of academic rank. They do this, because . . . well, really because no one really knows what they're doing. Because *both* the English professor and the history professor need to learn Postgres; because the undergraduate student from art history happens to be the only one who knows Django; because, actually, you *do* need to learn how to draw (or at least know something about design), and the designers are pleased to reveal their art to you, because you are starting to understand JavaScript.

These crisscrossed lines of influence may not sound very "disruptive," but in an area of scholarship where coauthorship is viewed with suspicion and collaboration is rare, the idea that you *couldn't* master everything necessary to create a digital archive or write a piece of software was a complete revelation. It forced scholars to imagine their activities in terms of highly interdependent groups. To succeed, you had to become like the Clerk in *The Canterbury Tales*; "gladly would he learn and gladly teach."[1] Working as a full-time programmer at IATH in the late nineties (while finishing a PhD in English) not only changed the way I think about computers in the humanities but changed the way I think about the humanities, and about higher education itself.

The truth about IATH is that these disparate groups of people had already come together; the sudden arrival of a server only made things easier for them. And today, the cost of infrastructure has flattened considerably. How much money do you need to *start* a center? Either none or whatever the beer costs at the bar at which you launch this idea. What sort of infrastructure do you need? The laptops you already have and the free wireless on offer at the local coffeehouse. What sort of service and outreach should you do? The kind that goes out and finds new members for this highly informal gathering of humanists—students, staff, librarians, faculty—who like to geek out together and drink.

Does this sound like too humble a start? This is the founding narrative of some of the largest and most influential centers in the history of the field, including Alberta, Stanford, Maryland, George Mason, Brown, Bergen, Göttingen, Oxford, and King's College London. It was also the story at Virginia. It is true that all these groups will publicly credit the extraordinary vision of a dean or some highly placed administrator, but in back of that narrative is something much more fundamental and necessary.

Once upon a time, there were two students in a dorm who decided to make a list of what was on the World Wide Web. Once upon a time, there was a guy in a café who thought it would be cool to organize his T-shirt collection. Once upon a time, there was a person who thought the student directory at his university wasn't very good. We are speaking, of course, of what would later become Yahoo, Flickr, and Facebook. I do not mean for a moment to dismiss concerns over the digital divide. Zuckerberg was at Harvard; Yang and Filo were at Stanford; Stewart Butterfield was already deeply enmeshed in the high-flying, insular world of start-ups. The digital humanities centers I mentioned above are all housed at large research institutions. But we should be careful not to draw the wrong conclusions from any of this.

What are always in short supply—in computing or any other area of intellectual activity—are good ideas. I applaud any and all efforts to help bridge the digital divide with things like "minimal computing" as articulated by people like Alex Gil, Jentery Sayers, Stewart Varner, and others, but (and these scholars and librarians know this better than anyone) access to resources is a necessary but not a sufficient condition.[2] Access to ideas—the sort that lead one to other, newer, better ideas—is the main thing, and such things rarely arise from solitary activity. Scott Joplin was a musical genius before he ever touched a piano, but that genius didn't suddenly manifest itself when he finally did. It took teachers, mentors, other musicians, and other composers to reveal a talent that is striking above all for its originality. And there is no contradiction here at all. Centers are people; so is "Maple Leaf Rag."

I don't want to say that everything magically falls into place once you have formed the basic community of people and ideas, but it's staggering how all of the decisions that so obsess people trying to build a center follow logically and inexorably from the evolving needs and expanding vision of more or less informal gatherings of like-minded enthusiasts. "It would be nice if we had a server." "It would be nice if we had a bigger table." "I think we need a whiteboard." "Should we go for that grant?" "I'm an English professor. How do you write a grant?" "Think of what we could do if we hired a programmer!" Before long, you're trying to get some combination of the words *institute, digital, humanities, research, project, center, initiative,* and *scholarship* into an acronym that isn't already taken.

Years ago, while working at a center, my dissertation director stopped me in the hallway and said, "Steve, be sure to treasure this experience. I've worked in this field a long time, and I can tell you: you may never see this again." I think he was right and wrong about that. He was wrong; I've managed to see it several times over the course of my career. But he was also right. It's easy to treasure the wrong thing about digital centers: to see the excitement brewing in a community of teachers, students, and researchers as a new opportunity for what we might do rather than as a way to affirm an amazing thing that has already happened.

Care of the Soul

I suppose every field of endeavor has its clichés, but surely professional librarians are owed some sort of apology for the way those of
us who are not librarians rely upon the Library of Alexandria as a
surefire way to inspire, instruct, cajole—and even to scold—those
who are.

It's easy to understand why this remains a valuable go-to subject
for nonlibrarians. The Library of Alexandria, after all, is one of the
genesis narratives of the West. In the beginning, there was a library.
Not only that, but it apparently had all the features of a modern library (including, as far as we can tell, cataloging and acquisitions departments, thus indicating the eternal nature of these units). It was
also, from all accounts, extremely well funded. An ancient rumor
claims that the library bore a Greek inscription—*psycheis therapeia,*
which translates to something like "place for the care of the soul" or
even "soul hospital." (It's possible that the inscription belongs to the
library at Memphis built by my ancestor Ramses II, but I am merely
speculating.) It is also, conveniently, a cautionary tale, even if most
versions of that tale are probably false. Some say that Julius Caesar
himself accidently set fire to the library during a visit. Others believe
a Muslim caliph ordered its destruction. No matter. Fire and religious
fanaticism, both being bad for libraries, serve to remind us all how
fragile the whole thing is.

There is one thing, though, that is lost in all of this, and that is that
the Library of Alexandria, as far as we can tell, did not have any actual
librarians. Not, at least, in the modern sense. It's not that the people
there weren't concerned with the organization of information—
access and preservation, as we call it today. They surely were. It's that
every single person we've ever been able to tie to the library was either a poet, a literary critic, a historian, an editor, an astronomer,

a grammarian, a mathematician, a translator, or some other kind of scholar—including the people who are known to have held the title of "head librarian." Being a "librarian" appears to have meant studying and interpreting the contents of the library. They did, of course, have people there to help librarians do that—people who looked after the scrolls, kept the lamps burning, fetched things, pointed out the bathrooms, and so on. They were called "slaves."

These days, it is taken quite for granted that librarians and scholars occupy completely separate spheres in a modern university. It's not that librarianship has no element of scholarship to it or that scholarly research can proceed without a close dependency on librarianship. The deep interdependence of the two roles is another thing that non-librarians are obliged to mention. Still, at some level, they remain sharply separate. And no matter what sort of pious noises the non-librarians might make, the idea persists. Scholars create scholarship. Librarians assist them.

What is most remarkable about this, though, is how recent a development it really is. You have to go forward many centuries—really, to the nineteenth century—before you find the kind of strict compartmentalization we see today. We can go on and on about the importance of libraries to the contemporary university, but in the end, the library is considered a "service unit."

I think this is a terrible mistake.

I have been invited to serve as a consultant on the creation of digital humanities centers many times. Not once have I have ever been asked where this "center-initiative-thingy we're sort of imagining should be." It is always, always either in the library or closely associated with it.

How fitting! Because of all scholarly pursuits, digital humanities most clearly represents the spirit that animated the ancient foundations at Alexandria, Pergamum, and Memphis; the great monastic libraries of the Middle Ages; and even the first research libraries of the German Enlightenment. It is obsessed with varieties of representation, the organization of knowledge, the technology of communication and dissemination, and the production of useful tools for scholarly inquiry. But digital humanities is also, itself, a scholarly activity concerned not just with presenting knowledge or helping to locate it but with creating it. And it is here that the conventional, if relatively recent, configuration of the library as itself an assistive technology becomes a serious liability. Allow me to put the matter plainly: centers succeed when they allow scholars to act more like librarians and allow librarians to act more like scholars.

The alternative—a "center" that is really nothing more than another service point in the library for scholars interested in setting up blogs or creating websites—might curry some local favor. The university librarian can present that to the powers above as another way that the library serves the wider university community. And it's not a bad thing, certainly, to offer or to engage in such service. But most centers will never do serious cutting-edge research in digital humanities with this model. They will, at best, become places that are not falling too far behind.

Over the years, I've tried to offer the best advice I can. But in the end, I've just repeated the secret formula for becoming a place for the care of the soul: create a space in which the conventional separations among faculty, librarians, students, and staff become malleable—even, to use a term popular among hackers, "fungible." The good news is that computers—those wicked instruments that so deftly serve to make us all feel slightly foolish—can help with this simply by making us all a bit more humble in the face of the unknown. But in the end, it requires nothing more or less than imagination and leadership from academic department chairs and senior library administrators.

Here's some advice for the four stakeholders I just mentioned:

Library Administrators

Let anyone among your staff who is remotely interested in this center be part of it in some way. If someone knows how to program, or how to build web pages, or how to create databases, or how to make smartphones do miraculous things with GPS; if one of these people is way into some particular collection or some subject (and it can be anything from railroads to race relations); if any of these people have a wild idea for something digital: make some space for them to pursue that as part of the center's activity. Think of it as your skunk works. Think of it also as a way to let the extremely creative people who work for you be extremely creative.

Library Staff

Be persistent with your wild ideas. Given the million things that have to happen in order to keep a library running, it's at least sensible that an administrator would not want to let you get involved with something "extra." Of course, it's only "extra" until people realize just how brilliant it is. Then it becomes Proudly Sponsored by the University Libraries. Be patient. Alexandria wasn't built in a day.

Students

Digital humanities centers afford students—and especially graduate students—one of the few genuine apprenticeships in humanities education. They're a place to learn skills and methodologies, but perhaps more importantly, a place to learn how to become a professional scholar and researcher. If you're interested in this stuff, you should plan to do just about anything to be involved with one.

Faculty

Be prepared to be the least knowledgeable person in the room. Know, also, that being the least knowledgeable person in the room might be the best experience of your professional life. The greatest scholarly practitioners I have known in digital humanities were the ones who came prepared to learn, who were willing to roll up their sleeves, who respected the people around them, and who were committed to genuine collaboration. You can pull together a digital project by thinking great thoughts and then ordering people to "implement" them, but you'll never get a serious work of digital scholarship that way. Be part of it, and everyone around you will make you look good.

The most likely story about the Library of Alexandra is that it was not destroyed in some moment of avoidable cataclysm but that it gradually declined over a period of several centuries, and that no one thing led to its disappearance. That isn't the sort of story that makes for a good cliché, but it might contain the most important lesson of all. A library is, in the end, not a place or a thing but a sociocultural formation that, like any other such formation, waxes and wanes, thrives and declines, warps and weaves with the rest of the culture in which it finds itself. One shouldn't fear the world-historical processes of decline and fall that govern such matters any more than one should fear the fact that parents are ever destined to dislike their children's music or that the twenty-first century seems not to share the eighteenth century's fondness for death masks. One certainly should, however, ask whether friendships, alliances, communities, organizations, and the social forces and narratives that sustain them reflect the values of the people involved and whether older ways might not have been better than newer ones. That sort of *therapeia* is surely quite beyond cliché, even if it is, in its own way, a story we've all heard many times before.

Class Time

Who invented the classroom?

The question sounds a bit odd, because we who work in an ancient institution like the university are inclined to think that such bedrock notions as "the classroom" are likewise ancient. But in fact, the classroom was invented by a particular group of people at a particular moment in history, and in the scheme of things, that moment is relatively recent.

The main person behind this invention was the German Pietist educational reformer August Hermann Francke (1663–1727), who established charity schools in the German state of Prussia around the turn of the eighteenth century. Francke's innovations included the idea of a "roster" with which one could "take attendance" and the idea of "recess" (which originally meant not an hour of unstructured playtime in the afternoon but a set period in which students could work the fields). Other Pietist reformers invented the concept of raising your hand to ask a question and the idea of desks arranged in rows.

The purpose of these innovations was to stem the chaos that, from the standpoint of the Pietists, had governed the project of education for the better part of a millennium (Francke's first act was to shut down the thirty-seven taverns that had been serving the local population of two hundred—a beer-to-student ratio that makes most college towns look like temperance societies). But the underlying idea had to do with *time.* For most of history, the education that happened at a school happened in an entirely free-form manner. There were variations, of course, but generally, professors gave lectures more or less when (and where) they felt like it, and students likewise attended those lectures when they felt like it. Students might erupt with rude questions in the middle of an oration or stomp out in protest. Even the temporal boundaries of "being at university" were unclear; you went to school, usually as a young man, and, in the more extreme cases, left when you felt educated (or never left—a situation that admittedly persists to this day). Even the word *school* itself descends ultimately from an ancient Greek word, which, in addition to denoting learned discussion and disputation, was also the word for "leisure." And obviously, to speak of leisure is to speak of time.

The Pietist intervention put forth the radical idea that there was a time for listening and a time for speaking—a time for being educated and a time when that process would end. Having a roster and taking attendance was a way to ensure that time had been honored (time at your desk listening to the teacher). If you raised your hand and had the floor, you could speak. Otherwise, it was time for someone else to speak. Even recess was a commentary on time. Class was "in recess" in the same way that a law court is in recess: you might be allowed to do something else, but "the class" was still, in some metaphysical sense, in session. This allowed you to be "in a class" or "taking a class" even when you weren't, physically and temporally, there. Luther hadn't included Ecclesiastes in the table of contents for his 1534 translation of the Bible, but clearly, he and his followers had read it very carefully indeed.

These ideas about education and time are so firmly ingrained in the modern academy as to seem entirely immutable. Deans and provosts are glad to entertain various sorts of innovations in the classroom, but the idea of the classroom itself as something with concrete temporal boundaries is almost never in question (even in the most radical forms of "remote learning"). The really crucial thing is "contact hours"—an amazing term that unites the temporal with the physical. From the standpoint of a dean, reducing those numbers without authorization is not innovation but professional malfeasance.

I have, at various times in my career, had the opportunity to teach in classrooms that do nearly everything right in terms of instantiating the idea of a "digital classroom." Everything is on wheels, there are projectors pointing at every wall, there is a computer for every student, it has an audio system worthy of a multiplex cinema, and the professor can stand at a podium that recalls the bridge of the starship *Enterprise*. It is wired, configurable, comfortable, quiet, and intimate. And yet these spaces still occupy time. They still exist within a temporal framework that has seldom been tampered with in the last two hundred years. And what's odd about that is that it attempts to connect itself to a world in which time is being reconfigured in extremely radical ways. Think for a moment about "email time" or "Twitter time" or "Facebook time." The interactions here are not in "real time" (another astonishing phrase), and yet they aren't entirely asynchronous either. You have a certain moving window in which to "keep up with email" and a certain window before which you have to apologize for taking so long to reply. Wait too long to respond to a tweet or a Facebook update and the moment will have passed. None of these temporal windows is very precise, but the time in which you can respond is never "now or never." YouTube videos? Whenever you feel like it. Though eventually, the fact that you haven't seen the latest meme might catch up with you.

Contrast this with the temporal boundaries of the modern classroom. Class is on Tuesdays and Thursdays at 11:30. Do not be late. If you fail to show up, it might affect your *grade* (another innovation that dates to about the same period as Francke's classroom). The *homework* is due on Friday. The class begins on January 9th and ends on April 28th. You have until January 17th to decide whether you are going to continue to waste your time. After that, you're wasting mine. And that might be a bad idea, because this all about *credit hours.*

These aren't terrible ideas. Most ideas involving educational reform never find their way to an actual educational environment; this one has endured for over two centuries, and it has done so because, up until now, it has made a lot of sense. But does it make sense, if you'll pardon me, *now*? Does it make sense to create collaborative learning spaces (or whatever term we use in lieu of *classroom*) that are embedded in a temporal framework wholly unlike the ones in which they bid participation?

In the fall of 2020, at the height of the Covid-19 pandemic in the United States, I taught what was without question the worst class I have ever taught. In my department, we are asked to write reflections on every class we teach—short essays that are intended to do double duty as moments of pedagogical self-awareness and as postmortems for review committees. Of this class (a course on programming and software engineering for students in the arts and humanities) I wrote the following:

> I have taught this class many times (going back to 2001 or so). It has always been one of my favorite classes to teach, and I was looking forward to it last year.

When Covid hit, I immediately knew that there was no way I was going to be able to safely teach this class in person (I usually teach it in the DH computer lab in Burnett). At the time, there was a lot more concern about people contracting Covid through surface contact, and I just couldn't see how we could keep students safe in a close-quarters lab on shared keyboards. I wasn't opposed to teaching in person (and did teach an in-person class last fall), but I was certainly nervous about this one. So I petitioned to have this course moved online, absolutely believing that even without the safety issues, this was a natural fit for online teaching. I even suggested that it might stay that way permanently.

I'm really at a loss to express what a complete disaster this class was. I would say that maybe three or four students actually learned the material. Most people dropped it, and of those, many (if not most) did so because of plagiarism charges.

In the interests of brevity, I think I can say that the most fundamental problem was the fact that the students were trying to cram the material—maybe two hours' worth of extremely dense, complicated video lectures a week—and then trying to do the problem sets in the absolute final hours before they were due (students nearly always had several days to complete assignments). I did not, and could not, have learned to program this way myself; I don't think anyone can. I repeatedly pleaded with them not to do this—to please, please be attentive to time management and do a little of the work every day. The few who did that actually did succeed in the course, but most just flailed helplessly until they finally decided to just cheat.

I've heard from colleagues in the sciences (and in computer science) that they had similar troubles all semester, so I don't think I was alone. But at the same time, I don't think we instructors are entirely blameless. I think we (especially supposed "digital" folks like myself) overestimated our ability to teach technical subjects online. There is compelling research to suggest that retention from video lectures is low when those lectures are longer than *between five and eight minutes*; that many students treat video lectures as background to some other task (as terrible an idea with programming as it would be with a course on orthopedic surgery); and there is much that has to change fundamentally when you move a course online. I ignored most of that advice, and I think a lot of

people did (with devastating consequences for student learning). It
was a frustrating experience to deal with one plagiarism case after
another, but a humbling one as well. I honestly believe myself to
be a supportive and enthusiastic teacher who cares deeply about
students. But no amount of cheerleading, or individualized attention, or "pivoting" could get around the fact that students were not
engaging with a class that was not created with their engagement
in mind.

Years ago, there was much talk of online teaching in DH. In fact,
there was a general assumption among those in the "edutech" wing
of the field that it was only a matter of time before we all went to
MOOCs. Some even imagined that Covid, for all its misery, was
exactly the "singularity" that would make this happen.

I doubt there's anyone left who seriously thinks that. I, for one,
salute anyone who can teach well online (and I know there are
many such people). But this past fall, I discovered that I am not one
of them. Perhaps I could be with a good deal of reeducation, but
any illusions I might have had about how much work is involved in
creating effective online classes have been roundly removed.

Reading over that now, I can see that the experience was still a bit raw.
I have only slightly recovered months later.

But with the benefit of a bit of distance from both the class and
from my diagnosis of the aftermath, it is easy to see that the fundamental problem was *time*. Temporal terms abound in the paragraphs
above, and they range from the distressingly trendy "time management" to apparently innocent concerns with minutes, hours, and
weeks. The administration at my university (as at others, I suspect)
was very concerned with the distinction between synchronous and
asynchronous instruction. What I discovered, though, is that this distinction is mostly meaningless when the temporal framework of "the
class" remains firmly tied to conventional notions of "class time."

Purveyors of online courses (Udemy, Coursera, Khan Academy,
and so forth) offer a conception of class time that might seem similar to what universities offer through online degree programs, but in
most cases, the similarities are only superficial. As we all know, such
resources can be better than, worse than, or no different than the
considerably more expensive options offered through "real" universities. Nonetheless, there are striking differences. Typically, there are

a series of video lectures or presentations, chatrooms for discussion, and various quizzes and tests to gauge students' understanding of the material. But if you sign up for a course on linear algebra, or French, or music theory, there is not only no particular time in which you have to do anything (asynchronicity, as conventionally understood) but no time at which you have to *complete* the course.

That seems like a minor difference, but it recalls the chaos that Francke strove so assiduously to combat. You could watch eight lectures on French in one day (leveling up quickly, so to speak) but then take a detour into something else (say, modern ecology) at a more leisurely pace before coming back to French. Or not coming back to French. A few of the lectures on digital signal processing (a rather advanced engineering discipline) might make you realize you need a calculus refresher—actually, um, an algebra refresher, and then calc—but not the whole calculus sequence, because the digital signal processing class doesn't get too advanced until . . . later.

The natural objection is that if one doesn't *have* to engage with any particular thing at any particular time, what motivates a student to engage with it at all? But this objection only seems "natural" because we are heirs to the Pietist traditions of temporal order. What's more, the average professional scholar is every bit the anarchist in their own habits. "Lifelong learning" (there's a temporal term), for us, means deep dives into various books and articles, but it very often—perhaps more often—means skimming, skipping, perusing, failing to finish, and ignoring. We professional learners think of our own ongoing education as a self-guided tour through a garden of forking paths. At my institution, we try to get students to put their "four-year plan" in writing as quickly as possible and then monitor them carefully to see whether they are starting, stopping, and doing everything *on time.*

The self-reflection offered above should make clear that I am barely qualified to offer an opinion on either the efficacy of online learning or its methodologies. I'm not at all sure if our present way of doing things is right or wrong. I only know that it is entrenched—that every experiment, every innovation, every flip-chart-borne attempt to think outside the box about higher education tends to operate amid a set of assumptions that no one can seem to imagine changing. We speak of instruction as "asynchronous," but we don't really mean it. Or rather, we mean it in the small sense—on the scale of semesters (Pietists again, needing a term for six-month periods), or terms, or quarters. We do not ever seem to imagine our students becoming educated the way we educate ourselves—which is, indeed, the way they educate themselves outside of class on any number of subjects.

I will admit to being very hesitant when it comes to jettisoning the circle—that most ancient of all pedagogical formations in which people converse with one another on some topic. But beyond that, everything about "class time" seems to me completely up for grabs. Must the lecture happen in real time? Must "homework" happen outside of class time? Does everyone have to show up at the same time? Does everyone have to be "present"? Should the class end? Should it start?

Who's In and Who's Out /
On Building

[This rather infamous talk and its online successor—undoubtedly, and to my regret, the most oft-quoted thing I've ever written—was given to an audience of astonished spectators at the annual meeting of the Modern Language Association in 2011. Since it is by far my most well-known rant, I have reproduced it here without altering it in any way.]

Who's In and Who's Out

Kathleen has asked that we spend exactly three minutes giving our thoughts on this subject, and I like that a lot. With only three minutes, there's no way you can get your point across while at the same time defining your terms, allowing for alternative viewpoints, or making obsequious noises about the prior work of your esteemed colleagues.[1] Really, you can't do much of anything except piss off half the people in the room. As I said, I like it a lot. Here goes:

"Digital humanities" sounds for all the world like a revolutionary attitude—*digital* humanities, as opposed to old-school analog humanities. As such, it has most recently tended to welcome anyone and anything exemplifying a certain wired fervor. Nowadays, the term can mean anything from media studies to electronic art, from data mining to edutech, from scholarly editing to anarchic blogging, while inviting code junkies, digital artists, standards wonks, transhumanists, game theorists, free culture advocates, archivists, librarians, and edupunks under its capacious canvas.

Over the last year or so, I've heard lots of discussions—both on- and offline—about who's in and who's out. For the most part, people agree that having a blog does not make you a digital humanist. But beyond that, things are a bit fuzzy. Do you have to know how to code?

Does it have to be about text? Can you be a digital humanist if you've never been to a THATCamp?

"No, no, no," we all say. But we go further and say that it doesn't really matter. Everyone is included. It's all about community and co-mity, collaboration and cooperation.

But this, of course, is complete nonsense. Community and collaboration are undoubtedly signs of the spirit, but to say that disciplinary definition doesn't really matter is to eschew the hard reality of life in the modern academy. Digital humanities is not some airy Lyceum. It is a series of concrete instantiations involving money, students, funding agencies, big schools, little schools, programs, curricula, old guards, new guards, gatekeepers, and prestige. It might be more than these things, but it cannot not be these things.

Do you have to know how to code? I'm a tenured professor of digital humanities and I say "yes." So if you come to my program, you're going to have to learn to do that eventually. Does it have to be about text? If you go to, say, the University of Alberta, I suspect the answer might be "no"—a reflection, again, of the faculty, many of whom have been in the field for a long time. But what if Duke or Yale were to offer a degree in digital humanities and they said "no" to code and "yes" to text? Or "no" to building and "yes" to theorizing? Or decided that digital humanities is what we used to call new media studies (which is the precise condition, as far as I can tell, at Dartmouth)? You might need to know how to code in order to be competitive for relevant grants with the ODH, NSF, or Mellon. Maybe that means Yale's DH ambitions will never get off the ground. Or maybe Yale is powerful enough to redefine the mission of those institutions with respect to the humanities. Most institutions, for the record, are not.

Now, I've been in this game long enough to understand a few things about how disciplines develop. First, they really can destroy themselves through overprecise definition. That has already happened in classics, and philosophy may be next. You can also successfully create a polyglot discipline without schism (the average psych department successfully incorporates the tell-me-about-your-childhood psychologists and the slicing-open-rat-brains psychologists). You can also have a schism and have it not result in bloodshed (computational linguistics, a community now mostly separate from linguistics, comes to mind). But no discipline can survive without actively engaging with disciplinary questions. Not because there are definitive answers. Least of all because it's important to alienate people. But simply because without those questions, we cede the answers to institutions eager to oblige people who are paying attention.

Personally, I think digital humanities is about building things. I'm willing to entertain highly expansive definitions of what it means to build something. I also think the discipline includes and should include people who theorize about building, people who design so that others might build, and those who supervise building (the coding question is, for me, a canard, insofar as many people build without knowing how to program). I'd even include people who are working to rebuild systems like our present, irretrievably broken system of scholarly publishing. But if you are not making anything, you are not—in my less-than-three-minute opinion—a digital humanist. You might be something else that is good and worthy—maybe you're a scholar of new media, or maybe a game theorist, or maybe a classicist with a blog (the latter being a very good thing indeed)—but if you aren't building, you are not engaged in the "methodologization" of the humanities, which, to me, is the hallmark of the discipline that was already decades old when I came to it.

Am I right about this? With less than three minutes, of course not. But ask yourself this: Does having an opinion like this move us forward or backward? Is this a good fight or a bad one? Or is it better to let the whole thing emerge as it will? I say that the institutional structures in which we work have already decided in favor of having this discussion and that we can have it while still retaining our well-earned reputation for collaboration, cooperation, and good will.

On Building

I've said a few controversial things over the course of my career, and it seems to me that if you are so honored as to have other people talking about what you said, you should probably sit back and let people respond without trying to defend yourself against every countercharge.

But I'm worried that my late remarks at MLA 11 are touching a nerve in a way that is not provocative (in the good sense) but blithely exclusionary. The particular remarks are as follows:

> "Do you have to know how to code? I'm a tenured professor of digital humanities and I say 'yes.'"

"Personally, I think digital humanities is about building
things. . . . If you are not making anything, you are not . . . a digital
humanist."

I suppose I could say that both of those quotes are taken out of context, but given that all quotes are by nature taken out of context, it doesn't seem exactly fair to protest. But just stating things like this (as I soon discovered) really does touch upon a number of anxieties both in DH and among those who bid participation. I don't know if I can alleviate that anxiety. I'm not even sure that I want to, insofar as some anxieties can be oddly productive. But there's a lot more to be said here.

I've had the pleasure of talking with lots and lots of people in digital humanities from among a wide range of disciplines. And I've been having that conversation since the midnineties. I've discovered that there are lots of things that distinguish a historian from, say, a literary critic or a philosopher, and there are a lot of differences between 1995 and 2011. But to me, there's always been a profound—and profoundly exciting and enabling—commonality to everyone who finds their way to DH. And that commonality, I think, involves moving from reading and critiquing to building and making.

As humanists, we are inclined to read maps (to pick one example) as texts, as instruments of cultural desire, as visualizations of imperial ideology, as records of the emergence of national identity, and so forth. This is all very good. In fact, I would say it's at the root of what it means to engage in humanistic inquiry. Almost everyone in digital humanities was taught to do this and loves to do this. But *making* a map (with a GIS system, say) is an entirely different experience. DH-ers insist—again and again—that this process of creation yields insights that are difficult to acquire otherwise. It's the thing I've been hearing for as I long as I've been in this. People who *mark up* texts say it, as do those who *build* software, *hack* social networks, *create* visualizations, and pursue the dozens of other forms of haptic engagement that bring DH-ers to the same table. Building is, for us, a new kind of hermeneutic—one that is quite a bit more radical than taking the traditional methods of humanistic inquiry and applying them to digital objects. Media studies, game studies, critical code studies, and various other disciplines have brought wonderful new things to humanistic study, but I will say (at my peril) that none of these represent as radical a shift as the move from reading to making.

This partially explains why we have so long been accused of being "undertheorized." At its most sneering, this is a charge of willful exogamy: we're not quoting the usual people when we speak. But there's frankly some truth to it. As Geoffrey Rockwell wisely notes:

> DH is undertheorized the way any craft field that developed to share knowledge that can't be adequately captured in discourse is. It is undertheorized the way carpentry or computer science are. To new researchers who have struggled to master the baroque discourses associated with the postmodern theoretical turn there appears to be something naive and secretive about the digital humanities when it mindlessly ignores the rich emerging field of new media theory. It shouldn't be so. We should be able to be clear about the importance of project management and thing knowledge—the tacit knowledge of fabrication and its cultures—even if the very nature of that *poiesis* (knowledge of making) itself cannot easily (and shouldn't have to) be put into words. We should be able to welcome theoretical perspectives without fear of being swallowed in postmodernisms that are exclusive as our craft knowledge.[2]

Now that this scrappy band of naive gearheads are becoming the "cool kids," an anxiety that has also been around for a long time reemerges with new vigor: Do I have to know how to X?[3]

Most readers of this blog know that I have devoted my life as a teacher to teaching other humanists how to code. I do that for the exact same reason that others devote their lives to the study of Shakespeare or the American Civil War: because it's fascinating and soul charging. Like any passionate enthusiast—indeed, like any teacher worth their salt—I'm inclined to say that everyone should do as I do. But really, that's as far as it goes. Learn to code because it's fun and because it will change the way you look at the world. Then notice that we could substitute any other subject for "learn to code" in that sentence.

"Build," though, casts a wider net (and is, I think, a more useful candidate for X above). All the *technai* of digital humanities—data mining, XML encoding, text analysis, GIS, web design, visualization, programming, tool design, database design, etc.—involve building; only a few of them require *programming*, per se. Only a radical subset of the DH community knows how to code; nearly all are engaged in building something. *Procedural literacy* has been suggested as a substitute, and I like that term. Still, I think some of the people who use it are trying to answer the question "How much tech do I need to know to do cultural studies?," not "What is distinctive about DH?"

In the panel that set this off, Alan Liu tried to describe himself as not being a builder, but those of us with long memories know better. Because truly, we can date Alan's entry into the field (literally, as well as spiritually) to a very precise moment: namely, the day he started building Voice of the Shuttle.[4] Being a man of great range, he has gone on to do other very brilliant things (most significantly, in media studies), but I doubt very much if he'd be associated with DH at all had he not found his way to shop class with the rest of us bumbling hackers in the early nineties. He's one of many crossover acts in DH, and those of us with less talent are surely more honored by the association. One of the reasons the DH community is so fond of Alan is because we feel like he gets it/us. He can talk all he wants about being a bricoleur, but we can see the grease under his fingernails. That is true of every "big name" I can think of in DH. Every single one.

Now, some of my closest friends in the community bailed about five paragraphs ago, because they're sick to the teeth of this endless metadiscussion that another crossover DH-er once described as the "DH whine." They're especially tired of the "who's in who's out" discussion, and being generous folks, they're much more inclined to say that anyone can join. I feel their pain. And anyone *can* join (the "cool kids" metaphor, honestly, makes me worry about my career). If I had been less prone to provocation, I might have found a way to put things more positively. But in the end, I feel obliged to say that there *is* something different about DH and that it's okay to say what that something is, even if to do so is indirectly to say that some are doing it and some are not.

The Hot Thing

We asked the captain what course of action he proposed to
take toward a beast so large, so terrifying, and unpredictable.
He hesitated to answer, and then said judiciously:
"I think I shall praise it."

—Robert Hass, *Praise*

I find the *Debates in the Digital Humanities* volume terribly upsetting.[1]
Before I go any further with this dour and possibly inappropriate
thought, let me say that I find no fault with anything in the collection from a scholarly or intellectual point of view. There are many
superb essays in it: provocative, fascinating meditations on digital
humanities—defining it, theorizing it, critiquing it, practicing it,
teaching it, and envisioning its future. I think it will endure for many
years as the best testimony we have to what Matt Gold aptly called
"the Digital Humanities moment."[2] What upsets me is not any of that
but the ways in which the traces of certain deep fears and anxieties
emerge from nearly every page. It is by no means confined to those
authors who don't have tenure, or to those who don't have jobs, or
to those who don't have professorial positions, or to those who do. It
underlies, with few exceptions, the words of some of the most famous
people in the book, as well as those you may have never heard of. It is
to be found in praise as well as blame, and in the most earnestly dispassionate as well as the most overtly polemical pieces in the volume.

Because behind every utterance—including, for the record, mine—
lies the possibility of a terrible, soul-crushing anxiety about peoples'
place in the world.

Digital humanities is the hottest thing in the humanities. Who can
deny it? We read about it in the *Chronicle* and the *New York Times*. It
is "the story" of recent MLA and AHA conventions. Publishers are
falling over themselves trying to create new imprints and series in

the digital humanities. And there are jobs! Not many, of course, but many more, I would guess, than are available in any other single sub-discipline of venerable giants like English studies or history. So it is meet and good that we talk about this hot thing. But the question is this: Are *you* hot?

The answer to that question is "maybe." If you've devoted your-self to media studies, you *might* be hot. Your work is often solidly focused on the digital, after all. But when people say, "digital humani-ties," maybe they mean something different? And maybe they mean something that's *not* what you do? Maybe you're a theorist, in any of its many forms (including race and gender studies). Surely every form of discourse is capable of being theorized, and there seems to be a dearth of such theorization in digital humanities itself. But what if digital humanities isn't a fertile, open ground for theorization but a discipline hostile to it—or worse, the very thing that is slouching forward to *supplant* theory as a hot thing? Maybe you're just an ordi-nary historian or a literary critic or a classicist. You use computers, of course, and you're interested in what they might mean for the future of humanistic study. But what if this hot thing means that what you do—your work on *Paradise Lost,* or the French Revolution, or the writings of the late Roman Stoics—is now old fashioned, out of step, or even irrelevant?

The question likewise hangs over people who are, by all accounts, squarely doing digital humanities. You might have devoted yourself to something like data mining, or GIS, or TEI, or tool building. This, surely, is digital humanities. But then perhaps such things can't sur-vive the withering, highly articulate attacks of the theorists (or, for that matter, the old-fashioneds). Maybe this is just a passing thing. Don't you have your own doubts about it even as you engage in it? Maybe they're right; maybe the whole thing *is* subtly retrograde—even reactionary. It's undoubtedly *limited*—just one piece, just one form, just one thing, in the overall task of explicating the human record. But maybe it's not enough? And can it possibly live up to the hype?

Both forms of anxiety cross lines of seniority and position. I hear it in the words of old professors, as well as those newly minted, from full professors to staff. Graduate students and recent PhDs, it seems to me, feel it in the most profound way. Perhaps you were trained in theory or in some more conventional (and you *love* hearing that word!) form of humanistic study. You probably spent the better part of a decade learning to write a certain way, engage in certain kinds of conversations, and participate in certain kinds of scholarly activities. It took you years to do this, and it wasn't easy. Now none of that seems consonant with the hot thing. To be hot, some say, you must now learn statistics, document encoding, and C++. That should take you another ten years. And at the end of it, you'll be suffering from the same anxieties as the blessed. But not to worry: you won't have a job anyway, because you're *just too late.*

I am aware that by drawing a line between the contents of the *Debates* volume and peoples' fears and anxieties I am saying something that can be taken as extremely offensive. One implication of my observations is that whenever anyone is talking about one thing, they're really talking about another thing—that no matter how dispassionate and scholarly, no matter how concerned with the legitimate claims of probity and justice, scholarly "debates" are really just a reflection of some deeper personal conflict or worry. That's as likely to be well received as similar observations from one's parents (or one's therapist). And what's worse, these observations come from a *professor of digital humanities who has tenure.* Easy for him to deliver some avuncular homily about how fearful we all are!

I can only observe that among the obvious effects of this tension between the scholarly and the personal are good scholarship, provocative discussion, and excellent teaching. I don't think anyone can deny that, and I think the *Debates* volume demonstrates it amply. But there's another effect that we cannot deny: it can also produce bitter, angry people and broken communities. And I'm not talking here about the "DH community" (if that even exists). I'm talking about people in general, communities in general, and the uneasy lines of separation between them.

I entered graduate school (with vague intentions of becoming a literary theorist, incidentally) in one of the worst years for the academic job market to that point. Within a few years, I had wandered into humanities computing. I knew, almost immediately, that this was where my heart lies. I also knew that I would almost certainly not get a job in it. There weren't any jobs in it! It wasn't the hot thing, because it was barely a thing at all. I would love to say that despite all of this, I could clearly see that this was the future of the humanities and that, by memorizing the Java API, I was positioning myself for a promising academic future. I would also like to say that it was through several prescient acts of personal brilliance and productivity that I was able to land a high-profile academic position (with tenure) at a research institution.

The truth is that I figured that since academia wasn't going to work out, I might as well follow my bliss. I settled into what we now call an "alt-ac" job—with absolute joy, because that job was every bit as intellectually stimulating and exciting as the one I have now. On a lark, I applied to one of the first explicit jobs in "humanities computing" that, to my knowledge, had ever been offered in the United States. And I got it! Within a few years, I was being recruited by another institution that was building an entire program in, of all things, digital humanities.

So yes: easy for me to say. It all worked out. Yet it didn't save me from crushing amounts of fear and anxiety throughout the entire process. People have asked me "how I did it." The answer, as you can see, is not entirely satisfying. And because it is not satisfying, I have found myself asking a question that I've been asking for a long time, but now with greater urgency: How do you keep from becoming fearful and anxious—and possibly infecting larger communities with bitterness and anger—while going through this process, whether it works out or not? Because we have to confront the fact that there are highly successful scholars—those who appear to have ridden the "hot thing" to the highest levels of professional achievement—who are terribly bitter and who live in constant fear that it will be taken away. There are likewise people for whom it didn't work out at all (at least, not in the way we think of it working out) who seem happy and content. And, of course, there is the reverse of these as well.

One answer might be to be as "nice" as you can and take the world as it is. But I, personally, don't require the people who, as I said, are arguing on behalf of the legitimate claims of probity and justice to "be nice" about it, and nothing is ever accomplished in this realm by accepting the world as it is. Another answer might be to "follow your bliss," but it won't be bliss if you live in a constant state of worry and anxiety that this is precisely the way to end your career. I don't have good answers, here, though I'm inclined to think that Levinas was right and that "ethics is the first philosophy."[3] Despite some terrible associations, the word *benevolence,* which joins the concept of the "good" with the verb *to will* or *to wish,* encapsulates what I think makes communities healthy and what facilitates meaningful inter-action among people within a community and across different com-munities. You don't always have to be "nice" to be benevolent. Nor do you have to suppress the more productive forms of anxiety and frustration (because these do exist) that can lead to good and useful work. The fundamental posture of a benevolent community is that it wishes its own members—and, more importantly, the people who are not members—well. It doesn't unduly concern itself with its own survival or even its precise definition. And it doesn't concern itself at all with the idea that it will one day be supplanted by something else. It wishes the people it is "supplanting" well; it wishes the people that will supplant it well. And it wishes anyone who bids participation well. It might ask that people who want to participate take some time to learn what it's about, but it doesn't get overly exercised when this doesn't happen (and people acting benevolently will want to do that anyway). But most of all, it doesn't insist that people who are not do-ing the hot thing do the hot thing. This is the hardest thing of all, but I honestly think that communities cannot survive without this.

I, certainly, have not always acted this way, and yet I continue to think that the will for the good in others—first in thought, but ulti-mately in action—is both a radical possibility of the human person and the basis of any coherent call for tolerance, openness, and accep-tance. And we all know how to bring this about, because as teachers, we implicitly acknowledge the impossibility of a pedagogy that can proceed without this fundamental disposition. We teach *because* we wish our students well. Even when they fail. Even when they resist. *Especially* when they do these things.

So really, I need to qualify my initial statement yet again. I find the *Debates in the Digital Humanities* volume completely uplifting. Not because it shows no signs of the anxieties I've mentioned, but be-cause "debate" always holds out the possibility that benevolence will be the result.

I wish it well.

Notes

Preface and Acknowledgments

1. *Memory and Imagination: New Pathways to the Library of Congress,* directed by Michael R. Lawrence (1991), DVD.

2. Matthew K. Gold, "The Digital Humanities Moment," in *Debates in the Digital Humanities,* ed. Matthew K. Gold (Minneapolis: University of Minnesota Press, 2012), ix.

Textual Behavior in the Human Male

1. Alfred C. Kinsey, Wardell B. Pomeroy, and Clyde E. Martin, *Sexual Behavior in the Human Male* (Philadelphia: Saunders, 1948), 365.

2. Kinsey, Pomeroy, and Martin, *Sexual Behavior in the Human Male,* 369.

3. Kinsey, Pomeroy, and Martin, 369.

4. Alfred Appel Jr., "An Interview with Vladimir Nabokov," *Wisconsin Studies in Contemporary Literature* 8, no. 2 (1967): 130.

5. Ian F. McNeely and Lisa Wolverton, *Reinventing Knowledge: From Alexandria to the Internet* (New York: W. W. Norton, 2009), 229–30.

6. McNeely and Wolverton, *Reinventing Knowledge,* 230.

7. McNeely and Wolverton, 217.

8. Susan Hockey, *Electronic Texts in the Humanities* (Oxford: Oxford University Press, 2000), 66.

9. Jonathan Gottschall, "Measure for Measure," *Boston Globe,* May 11, 2008.

10. David Hoover, "Another Perspective on Vocabulary Richness," *Computers and the Humanities* 37 (2003): 152.

11. David Hoover, "The End of the Irrelevant Text: Electronic Texts, Linguistics, and Literary Theory," *Digital Humanities Quarterly* 1, no. 2 (2007), http://www.digitalhumanities.org/dhq/.

12. Stephen Ramsay, *Reading Machines: Toward an Algorithmic Criticism* (Urbana: University of Illinois Press, 2011), 9–10.

13. Haimin Lee, "15 Years of Google Books," *Keyword,* https://www.blog .google/.

Data and Interpretation

1. FOUND Magazine, http://foundmagazine.com/.

2. *Pareidoilie* first appears in an 1866 article by Karl Ludwig Kahlbaum, "On Delusion of the Senses" ("Die Sinnesdelierien. Ein Beitrag zur klinischen Erweiterung der psychiatrischen Symptomatologie und zur physiologischen Psychologie," *Allgemeine Zeitschrift für Psychiatrie und psychisch-gerichtliche Medicin* 23 [1866]: 1–86); *Apophänie* in an article by Klaus Konrad on the beginning stages of schizophrenia (*Die beginnende Schizophrenie; Versuch einer Gestaltanalyse des Wahns* [Stuttgart, Germany: Thieme, 1958]).

3. "He began, he recalled in 1996, to notice men in red neckties around the MIT campus. The men seemed to be signaling to him. . . . At some point, Nash concluded that the men in red ties were part of a definite pattern." See Sylvia Nasar, *A Beautiful Mind* (New York: Simon & Schuster, 2011), 242.

4. Plato, *Cratylus* 383b.

5. The customary phrase for demonstrating the problem of multiple generality as treated in Frege's *Begriffsschrift* (1879).

6. Bertrand Russell, "On Denoting," *Mind: A Quarterly Review of Philosophy* 14 (1905): 483.

7. David Kaplan, "On the Logic of Demonstratives," *Journal of Philosophical Logic* 8, no. 1 (1979): 82.

8. Noam Chomsky, *Syntactic Structures,* 2nd ed. (1957; Berlin: Mouton, 2002), 15.

9. It should be noted that "random data," or "noise"—both of which have a variety of concrete uses in any number of discourses and technical procedures—do not automatically fall within this category.

10. I'm thinking of Wittgenstein's gnomic statements at the beginning and the end of the *Tractatus*—in particular, "anyone who understands me eventually recognizes [my propositions] as nonsense." Ludwig Wittgenstein, *Tractatus Logico-Philosophicus* (London: Routledge, 1994), 74. But see Cora Diamond on the ways in which these statements anticipate the more explicitly antifoundationalist view of meaning in Wittgenstein's later work in "Throwing Away the Ladder," in *The Realistic Spirit: Wittgenstein, Philosophy, and the Mind* (Cambridge, Mass.: MIT Press, 1991), 179–204.

11. Lev Manovich, *The Language of New Media* (Cambridge, Mass.: MIT Press, 2001), 225 (emphasis added).

12. Brian Vickers, "Infecting the Teller: The Failure of a Mathematical Approach to Shakespeare's Authorship," *Times Literary Supplement,* April 17, 2020, https://www.the-tls.co.uk/.

13. Vickers, "Infecting the Teller."

14. Adam Kirsch, "Technology Is Taking Over English Departments," *New Republic,* May 2, 2014.

15. Timothy Brennan, "The Digital-Humanities Bust," *Chronicle of Higher Education* 64, no. 8, October 15, 2017.

16. Stephen Marche, "Literature Is Not Data: Against Digital Humanities," *Los Angeles Review of Books,* October 28, 2012.

17. Gao Ge et al., "Neural Metaphor Detection in Context," in *Proceedings of the 2018 Conference on Empirical Methods in Natural Language Processing* (Brussels: Association for Computational Linguistics, 2018), 607.

18. Richard Taruskin, "Last Thoughts First," in *Text and Act: Essays on Music and Performance* (New York: Oxford University Press, 1995), 5.

19. Aaron Copland, *What to Listen for in Music* (New York: McGraw Hill, 1957), 264–75.

20. Franco Moretti and Alberto Piazza, *Graphs, Maps, Trees: Abstract Models for Literary History* (London: Verso, 2007), 30.

How to Do Things (to Texts) with Computers

1. Keith Devlin, *Mathematics: The Science of Patterns* (New York: W. H. Freeman & Co., 1994), 1.

2. J. F. Burrows and D. H. Craig, "Lyrical Drama and the 'Turbid Montebanks': Styles of Dialogue in Romantic and Renaissance Tragedy," *Computers and the Humanities* 28 (1994): 63–86.

3. Louis Millic, "Unconscious Ordering in the Prose of Swift," in *The Computer and Literary Style,* Kent Studies in English 2 (Kent, Ohio: Kent State University Press, 1966), 79–106.

4. Susan Hockey, *Electronic Texts in the Humanities* (Oxford: Oxford University Press, 2000), 66.

5. Steven Lubar, "'Do Not Fold, Spindle, or Mutilate': A Cultural History of the Punch Card," *Journal of American Culture* 15, no. 4 (1992): 44.

6. Königsberg is now the Russian city of Kaliningrad on the Baltic Sea.

7. Leonhard Euler, "Solutio Problematis ad Geometriam Situs Pertinentis," *Commentarii academiae scientiarum Petropolitanae* 8 (1741): 129.

8. Of course, the starting and end points could be the same, in which case every point would have to have an even number of lines leading away from it.

9. This approach to the play goes back at least to Hazlitt's *Characters of Shakespeare's Plays* (1817). Harley Granville-Barker's *Prefaces to Shakespeare* (1927), in which the opposition of Rome and Egypt is put forth as the main organizing principle of the play's structure, might be said to inaugurate the modern discussion.

10. This graph was generated using a custom-built program that uses Graphviz—an open-source tool originally developed at AT&T Research—for graph layout and formatting.

11. All quotes from *Antony and Cleopatra* are taken from the Arden Shakespeare (third series) edited by John Wilders (London: Routledge, 1995).

12. Susan Snyder has detected a more or less constant pattern of motion in the imagery of *Antony and Cleopatra* that harmonizes both with the notion of the real and the apparent and with the general movement from one state to the

other: "Shakespeare has set images of solid fixity or speedy directness against images of flux and of motion unpurposive but beautiful to express kinetically the opposition of Rome and Egypt and, through their incompatibility, the nature of Antony's tragic dilemma." See "Patterns of Motion in Shakespeare's *Antony and Cleopatra,*" *Shakespeare Survey* 33 (1981): 114–15.

13. Donald E. Knuth, *Fundamental Algorithms,* vol. 1 of *The Art of Computer Programming* (Reading, Mass.: Addison-Wesley, 1997), 6.

14. N. Katherine Hayles, "Artificial Life and Literary Culture," in *Cyberspace Textuality: Computer Technology and Literary Theory,* ed. Marie Laure-Ryan (Bloomington: Indiana University Press, 1999), 215.

The Hermeneutics of Screwing Around

1. Matthew Arnold, *Culture and Anarchy* (1869; New Haven, Conn.: Yale University Press, 1994), 5.

2. Thomas Jefferson, "To John Garland Jefferson" (June 11, 1790), in *The Works,* vol. 6 (New York: Putnam, 1905), 71.

3. Everett Fox, *The Five Books of Moses* (New York: Schocken, 1995).

4. Thomas Aquinas, *Summa Theologiae,* vol. 1 (Scotts Valley, Calif.: NovAntiqua, 2008), 1.

5. Will Durant, *Our Oriental Heritage,* vol. 1 of *Story of Civilization* (New York: Simon & Schuster, 1963), vii.

6. The site would go on to become Yahoo—a company that would achieve a market capitalization of over $55 billion within ten years of its founding.

7. Franco Moretti, "Conjectures on World Literature," *New Left Review* 1 (2000), http://newleftreview.org.

8. Gregory Crane, "What Do You Do with a Million Books?," *D-Lib Magazine* 12, no. 3 (2006), http://www.dlib.org.

9. Pierre Bayard, *How to Talk about Books You Haven't Read* (London: Granta, 2007), 84.

10. Peter Bayard quoted in Alan Riding, "Read It? No, but You Can Skim a Few Pages and Fake It," *New York Times,* February 27, 2007.

11. Peter Occhiogrosso, *The Real Frank Zappa Book* (New York: Picador, 1990), 31.

12. Frank Zappa, "Edgar Varèse: Idol of My Youth," *Stereo Review* 26, no. 6 (1971): 62.

13. Martin Mueller, "Digital Shakespeare, or Toward a Literary Informatics," *Shakespeare* 4, no. 3 (2008): 290.

14. Crane, "What Do You Do with a Million Books?"

15. Ian F. McNeely and Lisa Wolverton, *Reinventing Knowledge: From Alexandria to the Internet* (New York: W. W. Norton, 2009), 20–21.

16. Vannevar Bush, "As We May Think," *Atlantic Monthly* 176, no. 1 (1945): 101–8.

17. Roland Barthes, *S/Z: An Essay*, trans. Richard Miller (New York: Farrar, Strauss and Giroux, 1974), 5.

18. Barthes, *S/Z: An Essay*, 60.

Code, Games, Puppets, and Kleist

1. Heinrich von Kleist, "On the Marionette Theatre," trans. Thomas G. Neumiller, *Drama Review* 16, no. 3 (1972): 24.

2. Von Kleist, "On the Marionette Theatre," 26.

3. Nancy Cassaro, *Tony n' Tina's Wedding* (New York: Samuel French, 1988).

4. Alfred North Whitehead, *An Introduction to Mathematics* (New York: Oxford University Press), 10.

5. Of course, there was another kind of "disappearance of the author" going on in the early days of commercial computer games that was a quite conscious decision by the AAA game companies. By removing the names of authors from their titles, and thus effacing the individual labor of game designers, the companies could more easily manipulate their corporate brands (and perhaps pay the programmers less, since individual consumers would be unable to treat them as we treat A-list actors and directors). This is all certainly true, though I think I have a much more metaphysical "effacement" in mind.

6. Infocom, *The Incomplete Works of Infocom, Inc.* (Cambridge, Mass.: Infocom, 1984), https://www.mocagh.org/infocom/.

7. Henrik Ibsen, *A Doll's House*, in *Four Major Plays: Doll's House; Ghosts; Hedda Gabler; and The Master Builder*, trans. James MacFarlane (Oxford: Oxford University Press, 2008), 1.

The Art of DH

1. See "How to Do Things (to Texts) with Computers" earlier in this volume.

2. Susan Snyder, *The Comic Matrix of Shakespeare's Tragedies: "Romeo and Juliet," "Hamlet," "Othello," and "King Lear"* (Princeton, N.J.: Princeton University Press, 1979).

3. Matthew Kirschenbaum, "What Is 'Digital Humanities,' and Why Are They Saying Such Terrible Things about It?," *Differences* 25, no. 1 (2014): 51.

4. Debates in the Digital Humanities book series edited by Matthew K. Gold and Lauren F. Klein (University of Minnesota Press).

5. We create work under the name "Perlin Trio." More recent pieces are usually available on the web at https://vimeo.com/.

6. Johann Joseph Fux, *The Study of Counterpoint: From Johann Fux's Gradus ad Parnassum*, trans. Alfred Mann (London: Dent, 1965), 19.

Digital Humanities and Its Disconnects

1. Alan Liu, "Where Is Cultural Criticism in the Digital Humanities?," in *Debates in the Digital Humanities,* ed. Matthew K. Gold and Lauren F. Klein (Minneapolis: University of Minnesota Press, 2012), 491.

2. Liu, "Where Is Cultural Criticism in the Digital Humanities?," 495.

3. John Harley, *A Short History of Cultural Studies* (London: Sage, 2003), 157.

4. Harley, *Short History of Cultural Studies,* 159.

5. "Decolonizing the Archive," Adeline Koh, http://chineseenglishmen.adelinekoh.org/.

6. Todd Presner, "Critical Theory and the Mangle of Digital Humanities," in *Between Humanities and the Digital,* ed. Patrik Svensson and David Theo Goldberg (Cambridge, Mass.: MIT Press, 2015), 61.

7. Presner, "Critical Theory and the Mangle of Digital Humanities," 63.

8. Presner, 65.

9. Presner, 56–57.

10. Max Horkheimer, "Traditional and Critical Theory," in *Critical Sociology: Selected Readings,* ed. Paul Connerton (Harmondsworth, U.K.: Penguin, 1976), 219.

11. Presner, "Critical Theory and the Mangle of Digital Humanities," 56.

12. Presner, 56.

13. Presner, 56fn.

14. Tara McPherson, "Why Is Digital Humanities So White? or, Thinking the Histories of Race and Computation," in *Debates in the Digital Humanities,* ed. Matthew K. Gold and Lauren F. Klein (Minneapolis: University of Minnesota Press, 2012), 140.

15. McPherson, "Why Is Digital Humanities So White?," 144.

16. McPherson, 141–42.

17. McPherson, 148, emphasis added. The puns in these sentences refer to the notion of an operating system kernel, a command shell, register-machine architectures, the software engineering principle known as SoC (separation of concerns), and the notion of "nearest neighbor" (which informs a dozen or so algorithms in computer science).

18. McPherson, 149.

19. McPherson, 153.

20. Mark C. Marino, "Critical Code Studies," *Electronic Book Review,* December 4, 2006, https://electronicbookreview.com/essay/critical-code-studies/.

21. Mark C. Marino, "Disrupting Heteronormative Codes: When Cylons in Slash Goggles Ogle AnnaKournikova," *Digital Arts and Culture,* 2009, https://escholarship.org/uc/item/09q9mokn.

22. Marino, "Disrupting Heteronormative Codes."

23. Marino.

24. Wittgenstein's detailed discussion of the distinction between "seeing that" and "seeing as" takes up a good portion of the second part of *Philosophical Investigations*.

25. Liu, "Where Is Cultural Criticism in the Digital Humanities?," 491.

As We May Not Think

1. See, for example, Anthony Grafton, "The World in a Room: Renaissance Histories of Art and Nature," in *Worlds Made by Words: Scholarship and Community in the Modern West,* 79–97 (Cambridge, Mass.: Harvard University Press, 2009).

2. Steve Schwartz, "No One Knows What the F*** They're Doing (or, 'The 3 Types of Knowledge')," Bridge Global, May 13, 2010, https://www.bridge-global.com/blog/3-types-of-knowledge/.

3. "RUMSFELD / KNOWNS," December 12, 2002, CNN, https://collection.cnn.com.

4. Slavoj Žižek, "What Rumsfeld Doesn't Know That He Knows about Abu Ghraib," *In These Times,* June 2004, 32.

5. Willard V. Quine, "On What There Is," *Review of Metaphysics* 2, no. 5 (1948): 21.

6. Schwartz, "No One Knows What the F*** They're Doing."

7. Matthew Arnold, *Culture and Anarchy* (1869; New Haven, Conn.: Yale University Press, 1994), 5.

8. In 2010, Google estimated the number of printed books to be 129,864,880 (Leonid Taycher, "Books of the World, Stand Up and Be Counted! All 129,864,880 of You!," Google Books Search, August 5, 2010, https://booksearch.blogspot.com/). In 2019, the Google Books project claimed to have digitized "more than forty million" volumes (Haimin Lee, "15 Years of Google Books," *Keyword,* https://www.blog.google/).

9. See Rich Hickey, "Are We There Yet: A Deconstruction of Object-Oriented Time," paper given at JVM Language Summit, April 18, 2009, Santa Clara, Calif.

Learning to Code

1. Alan Liu, "Where Is Cultural Studies in the Digital Humanities?," in *Debates in the Digital Humanities,* ed. Matthew K. Gold and Lauren F. Klein (Minneapolis: University of Minnesota Press, 2012), 491.

2. See "Who's In and Who's Out / On Building" later in this volume.

Stanley and Me

1. See Stanley Fish, "The Old Order Changeth," December 26, 2011; "The Digital Humanities and the Transcending of Mortality," January 9, 2012; and

"Mind Your P's and B's: The Digital Humanities and Interpretation," January 23, 2012, *Opinionator* (blog), *New York Times,* https://opinionator.blogs.nytimes.com.

2. Fish, "Mind Your P's and B's."

3. J. F. Burrows and D. H. Craig, "Lyrical Drama and the 'Turbid Montebanks': Styles of Dialogue in Romantic and Renaissance Tragedy," *Computers and the Humanities* 28 (1994): 64.

4. Louis Milic quoted in Stanley Fish, *Is There a Text in This Class? The Authority of Interpretive Communities* (Cambridge, Mass.: Harvard University Press, 1982), 71.

5. Fish, *Is There a Text in This Class?,* 72.

6. Fish, 72.

7. George Steiner, *The Death of Tragedy* (1961; New Haven, Conn.: Yale University Press, 2009), 8.

8. Fish, *Is There a Text in This Class?,* 72.

9. Fish, "Mind Your P's and B's."

10. Mark Liberman, "The 'Dance of the P's and B's': Truth or Noise?," *Language Log,* January 26, 2012, https://languagelog.ldc.upenn.edu.

11. Fish, "Mind Your P's and B's."

12. Fish.

Data Mining

1. Neal Stephenson, *In the Beginning . . . Was the Command Line* (New York: HarperCollins, 1999), 63–64.

2. Peter Ainsworth et al., "Digging into Image Data to Answer Authorship-Related Questions (DID-ARQ)," Image Spatial Data Analysis Group, http://isda.ncsa.illinois.edu/DID/.

3. Dan Edelstein, "Digging into the Enlightenment: Mapping the Republic of Letters," https://www.e-enlightenment.com/.

4. Mats Roots, "It's All in How You Say It: Cornell Linguist Studies How the Way We Speak Affects Meaning," https://news.cornell.edu/.

Centers of Attention

1. Geoffrey Chaucer, *The Riverside Chaucer,* ed. Larry D. Benson (New York: Houghton, 2008), 28.

2. See especially the various essays presented by the Minimal Computing Working Group, https://go-dh.github.io/mincomp/.

Who's In and Who's Out / On Building

1. Kathleen Fitzpatrick was the chair of the panel, which was entitled "The History and Future of Digital Humanities."

2. Geoffrey Rockwell, "Inclusion in the Digital Humanities," in *Defining Digital Humanities: A Reader,* ed. Melissa Terras, Julianne Nyhan, and Edward Vanhoutte (Surrey, U.K.: Ashgate, 2013), 249.

3. See William Pannapacker, "Pannapacker at MLA: Digital Humanities Triumphant?," *Chronicle of Higher Education,* January 8, 2011, https://www.chronicle.com.

4. Voice of the Shuttle, http://vos.ucsb.edu/.

The Hot Thing

1. The occasion for this brief talk was the launch party for the very first volume of the Debates in the Digital Humanities series in 2012 (edited by Matthew K. Gold and Lauren F. Klein, University of Minnesota Press).

2. Matthew K. Gold, "The Digital Humanities Moment," in *Debates in the Digital Humanities,* ed. Matthew K. Gold (Minneapolis: University of Minnesota Press, 2012), ix.

3. This phrase ("éthique comme philosophie première"), long associated with Levinas, is perhaps most clearly articulated in *Totality and Infinity: An Essay on Exteriority* (Pittsburgh: Duquesne University Press, 1969).

Index

Page numbers in italics refer to figures.

Stephen Ramsay is associate professor of English and Fellow at the Center for Digital Research in the Humanities at the University of Nebraska–Lincoln. He is author of *Reading Machines: Toward an Algorithmic Criticism* and coauthor of *Six Septembers: Mathematics for the Humanist.*